Encyclopedia of

UKRAINE

MAP & GAZETTEER

Edited by
VOLODYMYR KUBIJOVYČ

Published for the Canadian Institute of Ukrainian Studies,
the Shevchenko Scientific Society (Sarcelles, France), and
the Canadian Foundation for Ukrainian Studies

UNIVERSITY OF TORONTO PRESS
Toronto Buffalo London

Map printed in the Federal Republic of Germany;
cartography and printing by Karl Wenschow-Franzis-Druck Gmbh, Munich

Text printed in Canada at University of Toronto Press

ISBN 0-8020-3362-8
Collector's Edition: ISBN 0-8020-3416-0

Canadian Cataloguing in Publication Data
Main entry under title:
Encyclopedia of Ukraine

Revision of: Entsyklopediia ukraïnoznavstva.
Includes bibliographies.
Partial contents: Map and gazetteer volume. –
V. 1. A–F
ISBN 0-8020-3362-8

1. Ukraine – Dictionaries and encyclopedias.
2. Ukraine – Gazetteers. I. Kubijovyč, V. (Volodymyr), 1900–
II. Canadian Institute of Ukrainian Studies.
III. Naukove tovarystvo imeny Shevchenka.
IV. Canadian Foundation for Ukrainian Studies.
V. Title: Entsyklopediia ukraïnoznavstva.

DK508.E52 1984   947'.71'003   c84-099336-6

Map & Gazetteer of

UKRAINE

Compiled by
VOLODYMYR KUBIJOVYČ
and
ARKADII ZHUKOVSKY

Scale 1:2,000,000

Introduction

UKRAINIAN ETHNIC TERRITORY

Ukrainian ethnic territory, ie, the territory inhabited by Ukrainians, can be divided into (1) a compact national territory with a predominantly Ukrainian population, and (2) a mixed ethnic territory (Ukrainian-Russian, Ukrainian-Polish, and so on). From earliest times, as a result of the colonizing processes of nomadic peoples in the south and southeast, the boundaries and size of Ukrainian ethnic territory have changed substantially. In the early 13th century, during the Princely era, Ukrainian ethnic territory covered about 400,000 sq km. The Tatar invasions reduced this area to approximately 250,000 sq km and resulted in the relocation of its boundaries farther to the north. In the early 14th century, during the period of Lithuanian political expansion, Ukrainian ethnic territory increased. It decreased again, to about 280,000 sq km, towards the end of the 15th century during the second period of Tatar expansion. Intensive Ukrainian colonization of the forest-steppe on the Right Bank and subsequently on the Left Bank, as well as of Slobidska Ukraine and Zaporizhia, began in the late 16th century. As a result, Ukrainian ethnic territory grew to about 450,000 sq km by the middle of the 18th century. By the middle of the 19th century, with the settlement of the steppe region and the Kuban, this area increased further to about 700,000 sq km. The eastern Kuban and the Terek and Stavropil regions were also colonized by Russians. Consequently a large Ukrainian-Russian mixed territory arose in the southeast. As Ukrainian ethnic territory expanded in the south and east, it diminished, though not greatly, in the west and southwest, where it was replaced by Polish, Slovak, and Hungarian ethnic territories.

The size of the compact Ukrainian national territory in 1914 was estimated at 739,160 sq km with a population of 46 million: 664,630 sq km with 39.6 million inhabitants was under Russian domination, and 74,530 sq km with 6.4 million inhabitants was part of the Austro-Hungarian Empire.

The independent Ukrainian state of 1918–20 embraced an area of 690,000 sq km, including 60,000 sq km that had been temporarily annexed.

Using the Soviet census of 17 December 1926, Polish and Czechoslovak statistics, and other data, V. Kubijovyč determined that Ukrainian ethnic territory embraces 932,000 sq km. He subdivided this territory into two areas: compact – 729,000 sq km – and mixed (eastern Subcaucasia, the Crimea, the northern Chernihiv region, the Kholm region, and Podlachia – 203,000 sq km. The following table shows how Ukrainian ethnic territory was divided politically (the mixed territory is in parentheses) towards the end of 1938.

UKRAINIAN LANDS IN 1938

Country	Territory (1,000 sq km)	Population (millions)
USSR	564 (767)	37.7 (42.2)
Poland	132	10.2
Rumania	18	1.4
Czechoslovakia	15	0.8
TOTAL	729 (932)	50.1 (54.6)
Ukrainian SSR	443	31.9

During the Second World War, the territory of the Ukrainian SSR increased, with the incorporation of Galicia and western Volhynia in 1939, northern Bukovyna and parts of Bessarabia in 1940, and Transcarpathia in 1945. In 1954 the Crimea was transferred to Soviet Ukraine from the Russian RSFSR. Consequently almost all Ukrainian lands lie within the borders of the USSR today; 80 percent of the compact territory and more than 87 percent of the population are in Soviet Ukraine. The western borderlands of Ukrainian ethnic territory diminished by 19,500 sq km immediately after the war, however, as a direct result of the mass deportation and resettlement of the indigenous Ukrainian population from those areas that became part of the Polish People's Republic.

The unceasing Russification of all Soviet areas lying outside the Ukrainian SSR has contributed to the diminution of Ukrainian compact territory, and even more so of mixed territory. In general the western boundaries of Ukrainian territory now correspond closely with the political borders of the Ukrainian SSR with Poland, Czechoslovakia, Hungary, and Rumania, although small strips of Hungarian and Rumanian ethnic territory are found in Soviet Ukraine.

The following table shows the division of Ukrainian ethnic territory in 1970 (the data for Ukrainian lands outside Soviet Ukraine are only approximate).

UKRAINIAN ETHNIC TERRITORY IN 1970

Country	Territory (1,000 sq km)		Population (millions)	
I. Ukrainian SSR		603.7		47.1
II. Ukrainian compact (ethnic) territory outside the Ukrainian SSR				
1. Russian SFSR				
a) Belgorod, Kursk, and Voronezh oblasts[1]	43.9		2.5	
b) Don region[2]	23.8		1.0	
c) Western Subcaucasia (the Kuban[3])	46.6		2.9	
Subtotal (1)	114.3		6.4	
2. Belorussia[4]	27.0		1.0	
3. Czechoslovakia[5]	3.5		0.1	
4. Rumania[6]	1.7		0.1	
Subtotal (II)	146.5	146.5	7.6	7.6
III. Ukrainian compact (ethnic) territories in Europe (subtotal I + II)		750.2		54.7
IV. Ukrainian ethnically mixed territories				
1. Northern Chernihiv region[7]	14.2		0.8	
2. Eastern Subcaucasia[8]	163.4		4.6	
3. Ukrainian territory in Poland[9]	19.5		1.7	
Subtotal (IV)	197.1	197.1	7.1	7.1
V. Ukrainian lands in Europe (total III + IV)		947.3		61.8

1 Southern parts
2 The western part of Rostov oblast
3 Part of Krasnodar krai and a small southwestern section of Rostov oblast
4 Part of Brest and Homel oblasts
5 The eastern part of Slovakia
6 Small parts of Suceava and Maramureş districts
7 Part of Briansk oblast
8 The eastern part of Krasnodar krai, together with Adygei autonomous oblast, Stavropol krai, and parts of Karachai-Cherkess autonomous oblast
9 Parts of Białystok, Cracow, Lublin, and Rzeszów voivodeships. This formerly Ukrainian ethnic territory was settled by Poles after the deportation of the Ukrainian population in 1946–7. Statistics are for 1939.

ADMINISTRATIVE TERRITORIAL DIVISION AND POPULATION OF THE UKRAINIAN ssr
(as of 1 January 1983)

Oblast	Area (1,000 sq km)	Population (thousands)			Urban population (% of total)	Population density per sq km
		Total	Urban	Rural		
Cherkasy	20.9	1,533.3	733.4	799.9	48	73.4
Chernihiv	31.9	1,459.0	703.1	755.9	48	45.7
Chernivtsi	8.1	905.2	357.0	548.2	39	111.8
Crimea	27.0	2,276.5	1,570.1	706.4	69	84.3
Dnipropetrovske	31.9	3,746.6	3,078.0	668.6	82	117.4
Donetske	26.5	5,251.7	4,717.7	534.0	90	198.2
Ivano-Frankivske	13.9	1,360.1	539.5	820.6	40	97.8
Kharkiv	31.4	3,110.1	2,383.9	726.2	77	99.0
Kherson	28.5	1,194.4	716.1	478.3	60	41.9
Khmelnytskyi	20.6	1,536.9	620.5	916.4	40	74.6
Kiev (without city)	28.9	1,923.9	949.7	974.2	49	148.3
Kiev (city)		2,362.0	2,362.0	–	100	
Kirovohrad	24.6	1,238.3	685.8	552.5	55	50.3
Lviv	21.8	2,621.7	1,467.9	1,153.8	56	120.3
Mykolaiv	24.6	1,267.9	797.7	470.2	63	51.5
Odessa	33.3	2,587.6	1,660.7	926.9	64	77.7
Poltava	28.8	1,726.7	916.9	809.8	53	60.0
Rivne	20.1	1,149.5	467.7	681.8	41	57.2
Sumy	23.8	1,444.5	811.3	633.2	56	60.7
Ternopil	13.8	1,162.1	405.6	756.5	35	84.2
Transcarpathia	12.8	1,187.7	469.0	718.7	39	92.8
Vinnytsia	26.5	1,996.8	773.8	1,223.0	39	75.4
Volhynia	20.2	1,032.2	448.6	583.6	43	51.1
Voroshylovhrad	26.7	2,808.0	2,410.8	397.2	86	105.2
Zaporizhia	27.2	2,008.1	1,473.4	534.7	73	73.8
Zhytomyr	29.9	1,569.9	747.3	822.6	48	52.5
Total	603.7	50,460.7	32,267.5	18,193.2	64	83.6

CITIES WITH A POPULATION GREATER THAN 100,000
(in thousands)

	1939	1959	1979	1983
IN UKRAINIAN SSR				
Kiev	851	1,106	2,137	2,355
Kharkiv	840	953	1,444	1,519
Dnipropetrovske	528	690	1,066	1,128
Odessa	599	664	1,046	1,097
Donetske	474	708	1,021	1,055
Zaporizhia	289	449	781	835
Lviv	340	411	667	711
Kryvyi Rih	192	408	650	674
Zhdanov	222	284	503	516
Voroshylovhrad	215	275	463	485
Mykolaiv	184	251	440	474
Makiivka	270	407	436	446
Vinnytsia	93	122	314	350
Horlivka	189	308	336	339
Kherson	97	158	319	337
Sevastopil	114	142	301	328
Symferopil	143	186	302	324
Poltava	128	143	279	290
Dniprodzerzhynske	148	194	250	265
Zhytomyr	95	114	244	264
Chernihiv	69	90	238	263
Cherkasy	52	85	228	259
Kirovohrad	103	132	237	253
Sumy	64	98	228	248
Chernivtsi	106	152	219	232
Kremenchuk	90	93	210	220
Rivne	43	56	179	205
Khmelnytskyi	37	62	172	203
Ivano-Frankivske	65	66	150	189
Kramatorske	94	115	178	187
Bila Tserkva	47	71	151	171
Ternopil	50	52	144	168
Melitopil	76	95	161	167
Kerch	104	98	157	163
Lutske	39	57	141	161
Nykopil	58	83	146	153
Slovianske	81	99	140	142
Berdianske	52	65	122	128
Komunarske	55	98	120	122
Lysychanske	85	104	119	121
Siverskodonetske	5	33	113	120
Yenakiieve	109	117	114	117
Pavlohrad	40	46	107	115
Kostiantynivka	96	89	112	114
Krasnyi Luch	59	94	106	109
Stakhanov	96	91	108	109
Uzhhorod	30	47	91	102
Yevpatoriia	47	57	93	100
IN RUSSIAN SFSR				
Krasnodar	193	310	560	595
Sochi	71	127	287	304
Tahanrih	189	202	276	285
Stavropol	85	141	258	281
Novorosiiske	95	93	159	171
Armavir	84	111	162	167
Maikop	56	82	128	135
Piatigorsk	62	70	110	116
IN BELORUSSIAN SSR				
Brest	41	74	177	208

ETHNIC COMPOSITION OF UKRAINIAN LANDS
(data for 1 January 1933)

Area	Total population (1,000)	Ukrainians 1,000	%	Russians 1,000	%	Jews 1,000	%	Poles and Latynnyky 1,000	%	Germans 1,000	%	Others 1,000	%
I. Ukrainian SSR													
1. Ukrainian SSR within 1938 boundaries	31,640	25,470	80.5	2,900	9.2	1,720	5.4	500	1.6	430	1.4	620	2.0
2. Western Ukraine (1938) within Poland	7,150	4,730	66.2	40	0.6	705	9.9	1,570	22.0	65	0.9	40	0.6
3. Bukovyna and Bessarabia (1938) within Rumania	1,470	770	52.4	90	6.1	140	9.5	30	2.0	80	5.4	360	24.5
4. Carpatho-Ukraine (1938) within Czechoslovakia	760	465	61.2	—	—	105	13.8	—	—	10	1.3	180	23.7
5. Crimea	800	90(?)	11.3(?)	335(?)	41.9(?)	55	6.9	5	0.6	50	6.3	265	33.1
TOTAL	41,820	31,525	75.4	3,365	8.1	2,725	6.5	2,105	5.0	635	1.5	1,465	3.5
II. Ukrainian compact territory outside the Ukrainian SSR													
1. Ukrainian territories in Russian SFSR	5,610	3,700	66.0	1,695	30.2	10	0.2	5	0.1	30	0.5	170	3.0
2. Ukrainian territories in Belorussian SSR	940	740	78.7	5	0.5	100	10.6	80	8.5	5	0.5	10	1.1
3. Ukrainian territories in Poland	1,360	650	47.8	—	—	135	9.9	560	41.2	15	1.1	—	—
4. Ukrainian territories in Czechoslovakia	120	90	75.0	—	—	10	8.3	—	—	—	—	20	16.7
5. Ukrainian territories in Rumania	110	80	72.7	—	—	15	13.6	5	4.5	—	—	10	9.1
TOTAL	8,140	5,260	64.6(?)	1,700	20.9(?)	270	3.3	650	8.0	50	0.6	210	2.6
III. Ukrainian mixed territories in Russian SFSR	4,800	1,430	29.8(?)	2,975(?)	62.0(?)	35	0.7	10	0.2	55	1.1	295	6.2
UKRAINIAN COMPACT (ETHNIC) TERRITORIES IN EUROPE	49,960	36,785	73.6	5,065	10.1	2,995	6.0	2,755	5.5	685	1.4	1,675[1]	3.4
ALL UKRAINIAN LANDS IN EUROPE	54,760	38,215	69.8	8,040	14.7	3,030	5.5	2,765	5.1	740	1.4	1,970[2]	3.6

1 This number includes 442,000 Rumanians, 240,000 Tatars and Turks, 216,000 Bulgarians and Serbs, 161,000 Greeks, 134,000 Hungarians, 108,000 Belorussians, 105,000 Czechs and Slovaks, 64,000 Armenians, and 38,000 Caucasian mountaineers.
2 This number incluces 448,000 Rumanians, 260,000 Tatars and Turks, 217,000 Bulgarians and Serbs, 170,000 Greeks, 160,000 Belorussians, 146,000 Armenians, 135,000 Hungarians, 107,000 Czechs and Slovaks, and 70,000 Caucasian mountaineers.

Nationality	1926 Census		1959 Census		1970 Census		1979 Census	
	1,000	%	1,000	%	1,000	%	1,000	%
Ukrainian	28,550	75.4	32,158	76.8	35,284	74.9	36,489	73.6
Russian	3,055	8.1	7,091	16.9	9,126	19.4	10,472	21.1
Jewish	2,440	6.4	840	2.0	777	1.6	634	1.3
Belorussian	85	0.22	291	0.70	386	0.82	406	0.82
Moldavian-Rumanian	405	1.1	343	0.82	378	0.80	416	0.84
Polish	1,900	5.0	363	0.87	295	0.63	258	0.52
Bulgarian	205	0.54	219	0.52	234	0.50	238	0.48
Hungarian	125	0.33	149	0.36	158	0.34	164	0.33
Greek	125	0.33	104	0.25	107	0.23	104	0.21
Tatar and Turkish	205	0.54	62	0.15	76	0.16	91	0.18
German	565	1.5	23	0.06	?	?	?	?
Other	210	0.56	226	0.54	305	0.65	337	0.68
Total	37,870	100.0	41,869	100.0	47,126	100.0	49,609	100.0

NOTE: The current ethnic composition of Ukrainian ethnic territories outside the boundaries of the Ukrainian SSR, ie, in the Russian SFSR and Belorussian SSR, is impossible to determine. This is because since 1959 the Soviet censuses have presented the statistics of ethnic composition only for entire oblasts (krais) and Ukrainian ethnic territory embraces only part of oblasts (with the exception of Krasnodar krai). In addition, Soviet censuses deflate the actual numbers of Ukrainians, presumably to show that the boundaries of Ukrainian ethnic territory correspond to the actual borders of Soviet Ukraine.

NUMBER OF UKRAINIANS IN THE WORLD

Some 11 million Ukrainians (about 23% of the total number of Ukrainian people) live outside Ukrainian ethnic territory. Their number is constantly increasing (in millions): 1.2 in 1880, 4.3 in 1914, 6.3 in 1933, 11 in 1980.

In the USSR, outside their ethnic territory, Ukrainians live either in small enclaves near Ukrainian ethnic territory or in large enclaves in the Volga and Ural regions, Moscow, Leningrad, and other cities. This European part of the USSR outside of Ukraine contains approximately 3 million Ukrainians. Considerably more live in Asian regions of the USSR: some 5 million, mostly in northeastern Kazakhstan and neighboring areas of western Siberia and the Far East.

The approximate number (in millions) of Ukrainians outside the Ukrainian SSR – individuals of Ukrainian ethnic origin who live in various countries – is evident from the following table.

Ukrainians in	1933	1980
USSR	35.2	44.5[1]
(of this number in the Ukrainian SSR)	(25.5)	(36.5)
Poland	6.0	0.3
Rumania	1.2	0.15
Czechoslovakia	0.6	0.15
USA	0.75	1.25
Canada	0.35	0.75
Other	0.4	0.6[2]
Total	44.5	47.7

1 On the basis of official statistics: 42.3
2 Of this number, 0.2 in Brazil, 0.2 in Argentina, 0.05 in Yugoslavia, 0.03–0.04 in Australia, 0.03–0.035 in France, 0.03 in Great Britain, 0.02 in Germany.

TABLE OF TRANSLITERATION*

Ukrainian

а	a
б	b
в	v
г	h
ґ	g
д	d
е	e
є	ye initially, otherwise -ie (eg, Yerky, but Selietyn)
ж	zh
з	z
и	y
й	y initially, otherwise -i (eg, Yosypivka, but Stryi)
і	i
ї	ï
к	k
л	l
м	m
н	n
о	o
п	p
р	r
с	s
т	t
у	u
ф	f
х	kh
ц	ts
ч	ch
ш	sh
щ	shch
ю	yu initially, otherwise -iu (eg, Yurivka, but Liubotyn)
я	ya initially, otherwise -ia (eg, Yalta, but Kolomyia)
ь	' (L'viv)

Russian

г	g
е	e
и	i
й	i
ы	y
э	e

*This transliteration is used in the gazetteer only.

ABBREVIATIONS

C.	Cape
Can.	Canal
Geogr. reg.	Geographical region
Hist. reg.	historical region
Isl.	Island
L.	Lake
Lim.	Liman
Mt.	Mount
Mts.	Mountains
Nat. Res.	Nature Reserve
Pen.	Peninsula
R.	River
Res.	Reservoir

Ukrainian SSR

Chrk	Cherkasy oblast
Chrh	Chernihiv oblast
Chrv	Chernivtsi oblast
Dnp	Dnipropetrovske oblast
Dnts	Donetske oblast
IF	Ivano-Frankivske oblast
Khrk	Kharkiv oblast
Khrs	Kherson oblast
Khm	Khmelnytskyi oblast
Kv	Kiev oblast
Krv	Kirovohrad oblast
Krm	Crimea oblast
Lv	Lviv oblast
Mk	Mykolaiv oblast
Od	Odessa oblast
Pl	Poltava oblast
Rv	Rivne oblast
Sm	Sumy oblast
Tr	Ternopil oblast
Zk	Transcarpathia oblast
Vn	Vinnytsia oblast
Vl	Volhynia oblast
Vr	Voroshylovhrad oblast
Zp	Zaporizhia oblast
Zht	Zhytomyr oblast

Donets Basin

Db Dn	See Donets Basin map inset

Belorussian SSR

Br	Brest oblast
Hm	Homel oblast

Russian SFSR

Ad	Adygei autonomous oblast
As	Astrakhan oblast
Blh	Belgorod oblast
Brn	Briansk oblast
Dag	Dagestan ASSR
Kal	Kalmyk ASSR
Krd	Krasnodar krai
K-Bo	Kabardino-Balkar ASSR
Krs	Kursk oblast
Lp	Lipetsk oblast
Or	Orel oblast
Rs	Rostov oblast
St	Stavropol krai
Tm	Tambov oblast
Vlh	Volgograd oblast
Vrn	Voronezh oblast

Other countries

Mol	Moldavian SSR
Pol	Poland
Slo	Slovakia

A

Abazivka	IV-15
Abrau-Diurso	IX-18
Abrud	VII-4
Abyns'ke	IX-19
Achkoi-Martan	X-26
Achuieve	VIII-18
Adahum, R.	VIII-18
Adamivka	V-15
Adjud	VII-8
Adyge-Khabl'	IX-22
Adyk	VIII-26
Adzhamka, R.	V-13
Adzhamka	V-13
Adzhara, Mt.	X-21
Aeroflots'kii	VIII-14
Afyps, R.	IX-19
Afyps'kyi	IX-19
Agnita	VIII-5
Agrakhan Bay	X-28
Agrakhans'kyi Pen.	X-28
Ahoi, Mt.	IX-20
Ahrafenivka,	Db IV-6
Aidar, R.	III-19; Db I-5
Aidar	III-19
Aigurka, R.	VIII-24
Aihul's'ke, L.	VIII-15
Aiud	VII-4
Aiuta, R. Db	IV-8
Aiutins'kii	VI-21; Db IV-8
Ai-Petri, Mt.	IX-14
Ai-Todor, C.	IX-15
Akhtanyzovs'kyi Lim.	VIII-18
Akhtuba, R.	VII-29
Akhtubinsk	V-27
Akhtyrs'kyi	IX-19
(Akkerman) Bilhorod-Dnistrovs'kyi	VII-11
(Ak-Mechet') Chornomors'ke	VIII-13
Aksai	VI-20
Aksai, R. (Don)	VI-21
Aksai, R. (Terek)	X-27
Aksai-Kurmoiarskii, R.	VI-24
Aksai-Yesaulovskii, R.	VI-24
Aksaut, R.	X-22
Aktash, R.	X-27
Akttashs'ke, L.	VIII-16
(Ak-Sheikh') Rozdol'ne	VIII-14
Akshibai, R.	VI-24
Aktsiabrski	I-9
Alba Iulia	VII-4
(Alchevs'ke) see Komunars'ke	V-19; Db III-5
(Aleksander Grushevskii) Shakhty	VI-21; Db IV-8
(Aleksandrovskii) Prokhorovka	II-17
Aleksandrovskoie	IX-24
Alekseievskaia	III-23
Aleşd	VI-3
Alexandria	X-6
Alibei, L.	VIII-10
Aliiaha, R.	VIII-10
Alikazgan, R.	X-28
Alkhanchurtsk Can.	X-26
Alkaliia, R.	VII-11
Al'ma, R.	IX-14
Almaş, R.	VII-4
Almaznii	V-21; Db III-8
Al'ta, R.	III-12
Altukhovo	I-15
Altynivka	II-14
Alupka	IX-15
Alushta	IX-15
Amvrosiivka	VI-19; Db IV-4

Anan'iv	VI-10
Anan'ivka	VI-11
Anapa	OX-18
Anastasiivka	VI-19
Anastasiivs'ka	VIII-18
Anatolivka	VII-12
Andreikovychi	I-14
Andriievo-Ivanivka	VI-11
Andriievychi	III-8
Andriivka	Db II-3
Andriivka	Dn III-2
Andriivka (Zp)	VI-17
Andriivka (Khrk)	IV-16
Andriivka (Khrk)	IV-17
Andriivka (Karan') (Dnts)	VI-18
Andriivs'ka	VIII-19
Andrushivka	III-10
Andzhiievskii	IX-24
Anenii-Noui	VII-10
Anhelyns'kyi yerik, R.	VIII-19
Anna	II-21
Annivka	III-18
Antoniny	IV-7
Antonivka (Rv)	II-7
Antonivka (Chrh)	III-13
Antonivka (Vn)	V-9
Antonivka (Chrk)	V-11
Antonivka (Khrs)	VII-13
Antopil'	I-5
Antratsyt	V-20; Db III-6
Anykyn	V-20; Db III-7
Apostolove	VI-14
Apsherons'ke	IX-20
Arabat Bay	VIII-16
Arabat Spit	VIII-15
Aralsor, L.	IV-29
Arbuzynka	VI-12
Aresa (Oresa), R.	I-9
Archeda, R.	IV-24
Argeş, R.	IX-6
Argun, R.	X-26
Argun	X-26
Arieş, R.	VII-4
Arkhangel'skaia	VIII-21
Arkhanhel's'ke	VI-14
Arkhypo-Osypivka	IX-19
Armavir	IX-22
Artemivka	VI-19; Db IV-5
Artemivka	IV-16
Artemivka	IV-18
Artemivs'ke	V-19; Db III-5
Artemivs'ke (Bakhmut)	V-19; Db II-4
Artemove	V-18; Db III-3
Artsyz	VII-10
Arzhir	VIII-25
Ashchiozek, R.	IV-28
Askaniia Nova	VII-14
Askaniia Nova, Nat. Res.	VII-14
Assa, R.	X-26
Astakhivka, Db	III-8
Astakhove	VI-20; Db IV-7
Astrakhanka	VII-16
Astrakhan'	VII-29
Astrakhan Nat. Res.	VIII-28
Ataky	V-8
Atamans'ka	VII-20
Auly	V-15
Avdiivka (Chrh)	II-13
Avdiivka (Dnts)	V-18; Db III-3
Azarychy	I-10
Azov Can.	VI-21
Azov Lowland	VII-16
Azov, Sea of	VII-16
Azov Upland	VI-17

B

Baba Liudova, Mt.	VI-5
Babadag	IX-9
Babaikivka	IV-15
Babaiurt	X-27
Babanka	V-11
Babenkove, Db	I-2
Babka, R.	IV-17
Babruisk	0-10
Babyntsi	III-11
Bacău	VII-7
Bagaievskii	VI-21
Bahata, R.	IV-16
Bahata Cherneshchyna	V-16
Bahatyr, Db	IV-1
Baherove	VIII-17
Bahlui, R.	VI-7
Bahrynivtsi	IV-8
Baia Mare	VI-4
Baia Sprie	VI-4
Băicoi	VIII-6
Baidars'ki Vorota, Pass	IX-14
Baigora, R.	I-21
Bairachky, Db	III-5
Bakal'Spit	VIII-14
Bakal's'ke, L.	VIII-14
Bakhchesarai	IX-14
Bakhmach	II-13
(Bakhmut) Artemivs'ke	V-19; Db II-4
Bakhmutivka	V-20; Db II-6
Bakh'mutka, R.	V-19; Db II-4
Bakota	V-7
Baksan, R.	X-24
Baksan	X-24
Baksha	V-10
Bakshala, R.	VI-II
Balabyne	VI-16
Balaichuk, R.	VII-11
Balaklava	IX-14
Balakliia (Khrk)	IV-17
Balakliia (Pl)	IV-14
Balakliia (Chrk)	IV-12
Balan (Mol)	VI-8
Bălan (Rum)	VII-6
Balandyne	V-12
Baliasne	IV-15
Balkivtsi	VI-7
Balky	VI-15
Balmazújvaros	VI-2
Balta	VI-10
(Bălţi) Beltsi	VI-8
Bal'shavik	I-11
Balychi	IV-4
Balyhorod (Baligród)	IV-3
Balyklei, R.	IV-26
Balyn	V-7
Bans'ke	V-2
Banychi	II-14
Banyliv	V-6
Bar	IV-8
Baraboi, R.	VII-II
Bărăgan, geogr. reg.	IX-7
Baranivka (Pl)	IV-15
Baranivka (Zht)	III-8
Baranów Sandomierski	III-2
Baranykivka	IV-20
Baraolt	VII-6
Barcău, R.	VI-3
Bardejov	IV-2
Barmantsak, L.	V-25
Barmashove	VI-13
Barvinkove	V-18; Db II-2

Barylo-Krepyns'ka	VI-20; Db IV-7
Barysh	IV-6
Barysh, R.	V-6
Baryshivka	III-12
(Baryshpil') Boryspil'	III-11
Basan'	VI-17
Basarabka (Romanivka)	VII-9
Başeu, R.	V-7
(Bashanta) Horodovykovsk	VII-22
Bashtanka	VI-13
Baskunchak, L.	V-27
Batais'ke	VI-20
(Batalpashinsk) Cherkessk	IX-23
Baturyn	II-13
Baturyns'ka	VIII-20
Batyr-Mala, L.	VI-25
Bazaliia	IV-7
Bazar (Zht)	II-10
Bazar (Tr)	V-6
Bazavluk, R.	VI-15
Beclean	VI-5
Bega, R.	VIII-3
Beisei	IX-25
Beisuh, R.	VIII-21
Beisuh Lim.	VII-19
Beisuzhok Livyi, R.	VIII-20
Beisuzhok Pravyi, R.	VIII-20
Beiuş	VII-3
Bekhtery	VII-13
Belaia Glina	VII-21
Belaia Kalitva	V-21
Belaia Rechka	X-24
Bel'bek, R.	IX-14
Belgorod	III-17
Beli Lom, R.	X-7
Belie Berega	0-15
Belorechensk	IX-20
Belorussian SSR	I-5
Beltsi (Bălţi)	VI-8
Beltsi Plain	V-8
Belz	III-5
Belzets'	III-4
Bełżyce	II-3
Bendery (Tighina)	VII-10
Berda, R.	VI-17
Berdians'ke (Osypenko)	VII-17
Berdiia, R.	IV-25
Berdians'ka Bay	VII-17
Berdians'ke Spit	VII-17
Berdo, Mt.	V-6
Berdychiv	IV-9
Berheciu, R.	VII-8
Berehomet	V-6
Berehove	V-3
Berehove Hills	V-3
Bereka, R.	IV-17; Db I-1
Beren Lim	VII-25
Berest	IV-1
Berestechko	III-6
Bereşti	VII-8
Berestia (Brest)	I-4
Berestova, R.	IV-16
Berestove (Zp)	VI-17
Berestove (Khrk)	V-17
Berestovets'	III-7
Berettyó, R.	VI-2
Berettyóújfalu	VI-2
Bereza Kartuz'ka	I-5
Berezan'	III-12
Berezan' Isl.	VII-12
Berezan', R.	VI-12
Berezanka, R.	IV-10
Berezanka	VII-12

Berezans'ka — VIII-20
Berezdiv — III-8
Berezhanka, R. — II-7
Berezhany — IV-5
Berezhnytsia, R. — IV-4
Berezhnytsia — II-7
Bereziv (Brzozów) — IV-3
Berezivka (Vn) — V-9
Berezivka (Krv) — VI-13
Berezivka (Od) — VI-11
Berezivka (Khrk) — IV-17
Berezivka, R. — VI-13
Berezna — II-12
Berezne — III-7
Bereznehuvate — VI-13
Bereznyky — III-8
Berezova, R. (Kalytva) — V-22
Berezovaia, R.
   (Medvedyts'ia) — III-25
Berezovaia, R. (Chir) — V-23
Berezovà Luka — III-14
Berezyne — VII-10
(Berkovets') Mykhailo-
Kotsiubyns'ke — II-12
(Berkovets') Kotsiubyns'ke — III-11
Bermamyt, Mt. — X-23
Bershad' — V-10
Beryslav — VII-14
Besedz', R. — 0-12, I-12
Beshpagir — VIII-23
Beshtau, Mt. — IX-23
Beshterek, R. — IX-15
Beshka, R. — V-13
Bessarabia, hist. reg. — V-7
Bessarabian Upland — V-8
Bezdizh — I-6
Bezliudivka — IV-17
Bezopasne — VIII-22
Bezskorbnaia — IX-22
Bezsonivka — III-17
Biała, R. — IV-1
Biała Podlaska — I-4
Biała Rawska — II-1
Białobrzegi — II-1
(Białowieża) Bilovezha — I-4
Biarezina (Berezyna), R. — I-10
Bibrka — IV-5
Bicaz — VII-7
Bicaz Res. — VI-7
Bicaz Pass — VII-6
Biecz — IV-2
Bielsk Podlaski — I-4
Bihor Mts. — VII-3
Bila, R. (Aidar) — IV-19
Bila, R. (Luhanka) — V-19; Db III-5
Bila, R. (Kuban') — X-21, VIII-20
Bila Berezka — I-14
Bila Krynytsia — III-10
Bila Krynytsia — VI-14
Bilen'ke — V-18; Db III-3
Bila Tserkva — IV-11
Bila Tysa, R. — V-5
Bil'che Zolote — V-6
Bile (Krs) — II-16
Bile (Vr) — V-20; Db I-6
Bile (Ad) — VIII-20
Bile, L. (Br) — I-6
Bile, L. (Vl) — II-5
Bile, L. (Rv) — II-6
Bilen'ka, R. — IV-6
Bilen'ka, R. (Dinets') — DB II-4
Bilen'ka, R. (Aidar) — IV-20
Biłgoraj — III-3

Bilhorod-Dnistrovs'kyi
(Akkerman) — VII-11
Biliaivka — VII-11
Biliaky — IV-14
Bilka (Zht) — III-9
Bilka (Sm) — III-15
Bilky — V-4
Bilobozhnytsia — IV-6
Bilohiria (Khm) — IV-7
Bilohiria (Vrn) — III-20
Bilohirs'ke (Karasu-Bazar) — VIII-15
Bilohorivka, Db — II-4
Bilohorodka (Kv) — III-11
Bilohorodka (Khm) — III-7
Biloiarivka, Dn — IV-5
Bilokurakyne — IV-19
Biloluts'ke — IV-20
Bilopillia — II-15
Bilorichens'kyi — V-20; Db III-6
Bilosarai Spit — VII-18
Bilotserkivka — IV-14
Bilotserkivtsi — III-13
Bilous, R. — II-12
Bilousivka (Mk) — VI-12
Bilousivka (Chrk) — IV-13
Bilovezha (Białowieża) — I-4
Bilovezha (Białowieża)
Forest, Nat. Res., — I-4
Bilovods'ke — IV-20
Bilozerka — VII-13
Bilozers'k — I-6
Bilozers'ke — V-18; Db III-2
Bil'shivtsi — IV-5
Bilyi — VII-20
Bilyi Cheremosh, R. — VI-5
Bilyi Kamin' — IV-5
Bilyi Kolodiaz' — III-18 (Blh)
Bilyi Kolodiaz' (Khrk) — III-18
Bilyi Kolodiaz' (Blh) — III-19
Bilyky — IV-15
Bilylivka — IV-10
Bilyts'ke — V-18; Db III-2
Bircha — IV-3
Bîrgău Mts. — V-5
Biriukove — VI-20; Db IV-7
Birky (Pl) — III-15
Birky (Khrk) — IV-17
Bîrlad, R. — VII-8
Bîrlad — VII-8
Bîrlad Upland — VII-8
Bîrsa, R. — VIII-6
Biruința — VI-9
(Birzula) Kotovs'ke — VI-10
Bisca Mare, R. — VIII-7
Bisca Mică, R. — VIII-7
Bistricioara, R. — VII-6
Bistrița — VI-5
Bistrița, R. (Seret) — VI-6, VII-7
Bistrița, R. (Șieu) — VI-5
Bistrița Mts. — VI-6
Bistrița Aurie, R. — VI-6
Bitiug, R. — I-22
Bivol, Mt. — VI-6
Black Lands, geogr. reg. — VII-26
Black Sea — IX-11
Black Sea Nat. Res. — VII-13
Black Sea Lowland — VIII-10
Blagodarnoie — VIII-24
Blagodatnoie (St) — VIII-23
Blahivka; Db — IV-6
Blahodatne, Db — IV-2
Blahodatne, Db — IV-4
Blahodatne (Mk) — VI-12
Blahoieve — VII-11

Blahovishchenka — VI-15
Blaj — VII-4
Blażowa — IV-3
Blidcha — III-10
Błonie — I-1
Blyzniuky — V-17
Blyznytsia, Mt. — V-5
Bober, R. — II-8
Bobrov — II-21
Bobrovytsia — III-12
Bobrovyts'ke, L. — I-6
Bobryk, R. — I-7
Bobryk (Sm) — III-14
Bobryk (Od) — VI-11
Bobrykove, Db — IV-6
Bobrynets' — V-13
Bochnia — IV-1
Bodok Mts. — VII-6
Bodrog, R. — V-2
Bodrogköz, gegr. reg. — V-2
Boh, R. — IV-7, VI-12
Boh Lim. — VII-12
Bohdan — V-5
Bohdanivka — III-18
Bohodarove, Db — II-1
Bohodukhiv — III-16
Bohodukhivka — IV-13
(Bohoiavlens'ke)
Zhovtneve — VII-13
Bohorodchany — V-5
Bohorodyts'ke (Brn) — I-13
Bohorodyts'ke (Rs) — VII-22
Bohuchar — IV-21
Bohuchar, R. — IV-20
Bohuslav (Kv) — IV-11
Bohuslav (Dnp) — V-17
Boian, L. — IX-7
Boiany — V-7
Boiarka — III-11
Boikiv Lim — VIII-18
Boikivshchyna — IV-13
Bokova, R. — V-14
Bokove — VI-11
Bokove Platove, Db — III-6
Bokoven'ka, R. — V-13
Bokovskaia — IV-22
Boldești-Scăeni — VIII-7
Bolekhiv — IV-4
Bolhrad — VIII-9
Bol'shaia Kugul'ta, R. — VIII-23
Bol'shaia Kazanka, R. — III-25
Bol'shaia Martynovka — VI-22
Bol'shaia Orlovka — VI-22
Bol'shoi Ertil', R. — II-21
Bolshoi Gashun, R. — VI-24
Bol'shoi Gok, R. — VIII-22
Bolshoi Kalytvenets', R. — V-21
Bol'shoi Kuberle, R. — VI-23
Bol'shoi Lomovis, R. — I-23
Bol'shoi Uzen', R. — III-29
Bol. Polpino — 0-15
Bol'shynka — V-22
Bondareve — IV-20
Bondarivka — IV-20
Boniski Lom, R. — X-6
Borcea, R. — IX-8
Borhustans'ka — IX-23
Borivka — V-9
Borivs'ke, Db — II-5
Borodino — VII-10
Borodaivka — V-15
Borodianka — III-10
Boromlia, R. — III-16
Boromlia — III-15
Borova (Kv) — III-11
Borova (Khrk) — IV-18

Borova, R. — IV-19; Db I-5
Borove (Rv) — II-8
Borove (Hm) — II-9
Borovychi — II-6
Borovyk, R. — Db I-4
Borşa — VI-5
Borsec — VII-6
Borshchevo — I-14
Borshchiv — V-7
Bortne — IV-2
Bortnyky — V-9
Borynia — IV-4
Borysivka — III-17
Boryslav — IV-4
Boryspil' (Baryshpil') — III-11
Borzhava, R. — V-4
Borzenka, R. — II-13
Borzna — II-13
Borzna, R. — II-13
Bos'ko — IV-2
Botiieve — VII-16
Botkul', L. — V-27
Botnia, R. — VII-10
Botoşani — VI-7
(Bozhedarivka) Shchors'k — V-15
Bozhykivtsi — IV-8
Brad — VII-3
Brahin — II-11
Brahynivka — V-17
Brahynka, R. — II-11
Brăila — VIII-8
Brane Pole — IV-11
Brańsk — I-3
Branys'ko, Mts. — IV-1
Braşov — VIII-6
Brateş, L. — VIII-8
Bratkivs'ka, Mt. — V-5
Brats'ke — VI-12
Bratslav — V-9
Bratushany — V-8
Brazhkivka, Db — I-2
Brazhyne, Db — IV-5
Breaza — VIII-6
Brech, R. — II-13
Breusivka — IV-15
(Brest) — I-4
Brezei, Mt. — VI-5
Brianka — V-19; Db III-5
Briansk — 0-15
Briaza — VI-6
Briceni — V-8
Briukhovets'ka — VIII-19
Briukhovychi — IV-4
Brody — III-6
Brodyna — VI-6
Bronnyky — III-7
Bronnytsia — V-8
Bronyts'ka Huta — III-8
Broshniv-Osada — V-5
Brovary — III-11
Brovky — IV-10
Brusyliv — III-10
Brwinów — I-1
Bryhadyrivka — IV-18
Brylivka — VII-14
Brytai, R. — IV-17
Brzesko — IV-1
(Brzozów) Bereziv — IV-3
Bubnivka — V-10
Bubnyshche — IV-4
Bucha — III-11
Buchach — IV-6
Buchmany — II-9
Bucovăț — VI-9
Bucureşti [Bucharest] — IX-7
Buda — 0-14
Buda-Kashaleva — I-11

Budac, Mt. VI-6
Budats'kyi Lim. VII-11
Budionovsk (Prikumsk) IX-25
Bud'onnovskaia VII-22
Budy IV-17
Budzhak, geogr. reg. VIII-9
Budzaniv IV-6
Buftea IX-6
Buh, R. IV-5
Bug, R. I-2
Buh (Bug), R. I-4
Buhaivka, Db III-5
Buhaz'kyi Lim. VIII-17
Buhuşi VII-7
Buinovychi II-9
Bukachivtsi IV-5
Bukcha II-8
Bukivs'ko IV-3
Bukovyna, hist. reg. VI-6
Buky IV-11
Bulavyns'ke, Db III-4
Burdea, R. IX-5
Burnachka, R. II-22
Burnas, L. VIII-11
Burnaz, geogr. reg. X-6
Burshtyn IV-5
Burul'cha, R. VIII-15
Buryn' II-14
Busha V-9
Bushanka, R. V-9
Bushtyna V-4
Busiv, Mt. IV-2
Bus'k (Buz'ke) IV-5
Buşteni VIII-6
Busko-Zdrój III-1
Butenky IV-15
Buturlynivka III-21
Buzaky II-5
Buzău VIII-7
Buzău Mts. VIII-6
Buzău, R. VIII-7, VIII-8
Buzhany III-5
Buzhok, R. IV-8
Buzhora, Mt. V-4
Buzivka (Chrk) IV-11
Buzivka (Dnp) IV-16
(Buz'ke) Bus'k IV-5
Buzuluk, R. III-23
Bychawa II-3
Bychok, R. Db III-3
Byk, R. (Dniester) VI-9
Byk, R. (Samara) V-17; Db III-1
Bykivka III-8
Bykovo IV-26
Bylbasivka V-18; Db II-3
Bylym (Ugol'nyi) X-24
Byriuchyi VII-20
Byriuchyi Isl. VII-13
Byshiv III-10
Byshkin' III-15
Bystra, R. (Donets') V-22
Bystrytsia, R. (Dniester) IV-4
Bystrytsia, R. (Dniester) V-5
Bystrytsia Nadvirnians'ka, R. V-5
Bystrytsia Solotvyns'ka, R. V-5
Bystrzyca, R. II-3
Bytkiv V-5
Bzura, R. I-1

C

Cahul VIII-9
(Călăraşi) Kalarash VI-9

Călăraşi IX-8
Călăraşi, L. IX-8
Călimani, Mt. VI-5
Călmăţui, R. (Danube) IX-8
Călmătui, R. (L. Suhaia) IX-6
Carei VI-3
Carpathian Foothills, geogr. reg. IV-2
Carpatian Nat. Res. V-4
Casimcea, R. IX-9
Caspian Lowland VIII-26
Caspian Sea IX-28
Caucasian Nat. Res. X-21
Căuşani VII-10
Cavnic VI-4
Ceahlău, Mt. VII-6
Ceadîr-Lunga VII-9
Cehu Silvaniei VI-4
Central-Chornozem Nat. Res. II-16
Cernavodă IX-9
Chachersk I-11
Chaha, R. VII-10
Chaltyr VI-20
Chamarysy II-11
Chamlyk, R. IX-22
Chapaieve IV-16
Chapaievka (Kv) IV-11
Chapaievka (Chrk) IV-13
Chaplyne V-17
Chaplynka VII-14
Charukiv III-6
Chasiv Yar V-18; Db II-3
Chatalkioi VIII-9
Chatyr-Dag, Mt. IX-15
Chauda, C. IX-16
Chebotivka, Db II-7
Chechel'nyk V-10
Chechen', Isl. X-28
Chechva, R. V-5
Chęciny III-1
Chegem, R. X-24
Chehem Pervyi X-24
Chekhove IX-15
Chelbas, R. VIII-20
Chelbas'ka VIII-20
(Chelm) Kholm II-4
Chelnovaia, R. I-22
Chemer II-12
Chemerivtsi IV-7
Chepehyns'ka VIII-19
Cherek, R. X-24
Cheremisinovo II-18
Cheremkha I-4
Cheremosh, R. V-6
Cheremoshne III-17
Cherhiv, Mts. IV-2
Cherkas'ke (Dnp) V-16
Cherkas'ke (Dnts) V-18; Db II-2
Cherkasy IV-13
Cherkessk (Batalpashinsk) IX-23
Cherlena, R. V-7
Chermno III-4
Chernavchytsi I-4
Chernecha Sloboda II-14
Chernechchyna IV-15
Chernelytsia V-6
Cherni Lom, R. X-7
Cherniakhiv III-9
Cherniavshchyna V-16
Chernihiv III-12
Chernihiv Polissia, geogr. reg. II-11
Chernihivka VI-17

Chernihivs'ka IX-20
Chernivtsi (Chrv) V-6
Chernivtsi (Vn) V-9
Chernyn IV-11
Chernyshkovskii V-23
Cherten', R. II-9
Chervona Kamianka V-14
Chervona Motovylivka III-11
Chervona Sloboda IV-13
Chervone (Sm) II-15
Chervone (Zht) IV-9
Chervone, L. I-9
Chervonoarmiis'ke (Radzyvyliv) III-6
Chervonoarmiis'ke (Zht) III-9
Chervonoarmiis'ke (Od) VIII-9
Chervonogranitne III-9
Chervonogvardiis'ke, Dn II-5
Chervonohrad (Krystynopil') III-5
Chervonohryhorivka VI-15
Chervonooskil Res. IV-18; Db I-2
Chervonopartyzans'ke V-20; Db III-7
Chervonopopivka IV-19; Db I-4
Chervonozavods'ke III-14
Chervonoznamianka VI-11
Chervonyi Donets' IV-17
Chervonyi Maiak VII-14
Chervonyi Oskil; Db I-2
Chervonyi Zhovten', Dn II-6
Chesaniv (Cieszanów) III-4
Chetvertynivka V-10
Chigla, R. II-21
(Chilia-Veche) VIII-10
Chineja, R. VIII-8
Chir, R. IV-22, V-23
Chirokha, R. IV-3
Chişinău (Kishinev) VI-9
Chişineu-Criş VII-2
Chkalove VI-15
Chkalove VII-15
Chkalovka V-14
Chmielnik III-1
Chodaków I-1
Chograi, R. VIII-25
Chograiskoie Res. VIII-25
Chokrats'ke, L. VIII-17
Chonhar VII-15
Chop V-3
Chopovychi III-9
Chorna (Pol) IV-3
Chorna (Khm) V-7
Chorna (Od) VI-10
Chorna, R. IX-14
Chorna Kalytva, R. III-20
Chorna Tysa, R. V-5
Chorne, L. I-6
Chorniavka III-18
Chorniava, R. V-6
Chornobai IV-13
Chornobyl' II-11
Chornohora, Mts. V-5
Chornohuzka, R. III-5
Chornoierkivs'ka VIII-18
Chornomorivka VII-14
Chornomorka VII-11
Chornomors'ke (Ak-Mechet') VIII-13
Chornomors'kyi IX-19
Chornorudka IV-10
Chornotychi II-13
Chornukhy III-13

Chornukhyne V-19; Dn III-5
Chornyi Cheremosh, R. VI-5
Chornyi Tashlyk, R. V-12
Chornyi Ostriv IV-7
Chornyvody IV-7
Chor nyi Yar V-27
Chortivs'ka Skala, Mt. IV-4
Chortkiv IV-6
Chortkove IV-21
Chortomlyk VI-15
Chovhuziv IV-7
Chuburka, R. VII-20
Chudniv III-8
Chuhmak, R. III-13
Chuhuiv IV-17
Chuhur, R. VI-8
Chuhush, Mt. X-21
Chuhynka V-20
Chuhynka, Db V-20; II-7
Chuikivka I-15
Chukurova IX-9
Chulykivka VII-13
Chumaky VI-15
Chupakhivka III-15
Chutove IV-16
Chychkliia, R. VI-11
Chyhyryn IV-13
Chynadiieve V-3
Chynhul, R. VI-16
Chyvchyn Mts. VI-5
Chyzhivka III-8
(Cieszanów) III-4
Ciechanowiec I-3
Cimişlia VII-9
Cîmpeni VII-4
Cîmpina VIII-6
Cîmpia Turzii VII-4
Cîmpulung Moldovenesc VI-6
Cîmpulung VIII-6
Ciuc Mts. VII-6
Ciucaş, Mt. VIII-6
Cluj VII-4
Ćmielów III-2
Codlea VIII-6
Codru Moma Mts. VII-3
Comăneşti VII-7
Comarnic VIII-6
Comrat VII-9
Constanţa IX-9
Copşa Mică VII-5
Corneşti VI-9
Costeşti IX-5
Covasna VIII-7
Cracău, R. VI-7
Crasna, R. (Birlad) VII-8
Crasna, R. (Tysa) VI-3
Cricov, R. IX-6
Cricovul-Sărat, R. IX-7
Crimea, hist. reg. VIII-14
Crimean Lowland VIII-14
Crimean Mts. IX-15
Crimean Res. IX-15
Criş Lowland VII-2
Cristuru Secuiesc VII-6
Crişul Alb, R. VII-3
Crişul Negru, R. VII-2
Crişul Repede, R. VI-3
Criuleni VI-10
Cserehát Mts. V-1
Curcurbăta, Mt. VII-3
Curtici VII-2
Czarna, R. (Wisla) III-1
Czarna, R. (Wisla) II-1

D

Dabosna, R.	0-10
Dąbrowa Tarnawska	III-1
Dadynskoie, L.	VIII-26
Dal'nyk	VII-11
Danube, R.	X-6, VIII-9
Danylivka	IV-20
Danylivka	III-25
Danylivka, Db	II-1
Darabani	V-7
Darakhiv	IV-6
Dariivka, Dn	IV-7
Darino-Yermakivka, Dn	IV-7
Dărmăneşti	VI-7
Dashava	IV-5
Dashchenky	III-13
Dashiv	V-10
Daush, R.	X-23
Davyd-Horodok	I-8
Davydiv	IV-5
Davydiv Brid	VI-14
Davydivka	VII-16
Davydovka	II-20
Debal'tseve	V-19; Db III-4
Dębica	III-2
Dęblin	II-2
(Dębno)	III-3
Debrecen	VI-2
Defanivka	IX-19
Deikalivka	III-15
Dej	VI-4
Deliatyn	V-5
Demuryne	V-17
Demydivka	III-6
Demydove	VI-11
Denysiv	IV-6
Denyskovychi	I-12
Denysovychi	II-10
Derazhne	III-7
Derazhnia	IV-8
Derbetivka	VIII-24
Derevok	II-6
Derevychka, R.	IV-8
Derevyny	I-12
Deriivka	V-14
Derkachi	III-17
Derkul, R.	IV-20; Db II-7
Derla, R.	V-8
(Derman') Ustens'ke	
Druhe	III-7
Desna, R. (Boh)	IV-9
Desna, R. (Dnieper)	0-15, III-11
Desna	III-11
Deva	VIII-3
Devitsa, R.	II-19
Devitsa, R.	II-19
Devladove	V-14
Diachenkove	IV-21
Diachkin, Db	II-8
Diad'kivs'ka	VIII-20
Diakivtsi	IV-8
Diakove	VI-20; Db IV-6
Dibrova	II-10
Dibrova	II-9
Dihtiari	III-13
Dîmbovița, R.	VIII-6; IX-7
Dinets'-Donbas Can.	V-18; Db II-3
Dins'ka	VIII-20
Dins'ke	VI-18
Diohteve	IV-21
Ditkovychi	I-5
Dmitriev-L'govskii	I-16
Dmitrovsk-Orlovskii	I-16
Dmukhailivka	IV-15
Dmytrivka (Chrk)	III-13

Dmytrivka (Krv)	V-13
Dmytrivka	VI-19; Db IV-5
Dmytrivka (Mk)	VII-12
Dmytrivka (Zp)	VII-17
Dnieper (Dnipro), R.	0-11; VII-13
Dnieper-Buh Can.	I-5
Dnieper-Donbas Can.	IV-16
Dnieper-Kryvyi Rih Can.	VI-14
Dnieper Lim.	VII-13
Dnieper Lowland	I-11, IV-14
Dnieper Upland	IV-9, V-14
Dniester (Dnister), R.	IV-3, VII-11
Dniester Lim.	VII-11
Dnipriany	VII-14
Dniprodzerzhyns'ke (Kamians'ke)	V-15
Dniprodzerzhyns'ke Res.	V-15
Dnipropetrovs'ke (Katerynoslav)	V-16
Dniprorudne	VI-16
Dniprovka	VI-15
Dniprovs'ka	VIII-19
Dniprovs'ke	V-15
Dnistrovs'ke	VII-10
Doboshanka, Mt.	V-5
Dobroie (Lp)	I-20
Dobre (Mk)	VI-13
Dobrianka (Chrh)	I-12
Dobrianka (Krv)	V-11
Dobrinka	I-21
Dobrivliany	IV-4
Dobrogean Upland	IX-9
Dobroie	I-20
Dobromyl'	IV-3
Dobropillia	V-18; Db III-2
Dobropole	IV-6
Dobroslavka	I-7
Dobrostany	IV-4
Dobrosyn	III-4
Dobrotvir	III-5
Dobrovelychkivka	V-12
Dobrovillia	V-17
Dobrovillia, Dn	IV-2
Dobrush	I-12
(Dobrych)	X-8
Dobryn'	II-10
Doch, R.	II-13
Doftana, R.	VIII-6
Dokhna, R.	V-10
(Dokshukino)	X-24
Dokuchaievs'ke (Olenivs'ki Kariery)	VI-18; Db IV-3
Dolgoie	I-18
Dolgorukovo	I-19
Dolyna, Dn	II-2
Dolyna (IF)	V-5
Dolynivka	V-10
Dolynivs'ke, Db	II-5
Dolyns'ka	V-13
Dolyns'ke	VI-10
Domasheve	II-4
Domanivka	VI-11
Don, R.	0-20, VI-20
Don Principal Can.	VI-21
Don Ridge	IV-21
Donets' Ridge	VI-18
Donets' (Dinet's) R.	III-17, VI-22; Db I-2, III-8
Donets'ke	V-18; Db II-3
Donets'ke (Juzivka)	V-18; Db III-3
Donetsk (Gundorovka)	V-21; Db III-8
Donets'kyi, Dn	II-5

Dondoşani	V-8
Don (Donshchyna) hist. reg.	VI-21
Don-Medveditsa Ridge	V-24
Donskoi (Rs)	VI-21
Donskoie	VIII-23
Dons'kyi, Dn	II-8
Dontsivka	IV-20
Donuzlav, L.	VIII-14
Dorohoi	VI-7
Dorohoshch	III-16
Dorohus'k	II-4
Dorohychyn	I-6
Dorohychyn (Drohiczyn)	I-3
Dovbysh	III-8
Dovhe (Zk)	V-4
Dovhen'ke	IV-18; Db I-2
Dovhe Pole	VI-4
Dovhobychiv	III-5
Dovhyi, Isl.	VII-12
Dovhyi Isl.	VII-18
Dovsun, L.	VIII-25
Dovzhans'ka	VII-18
Dovzhok (Khm)	V-7
Dovzhok (Vn)	V-9
Dovzhyk	II-12
Drabiv	IV-13
Drabivka	IV-12
Drabivtsi	IV-13
Drabynivka	IV-15
Drachyntsi	V-6
Dragomirovo	X-6
Drahove	V-4
Drobysheve	IV-18; Db I-3
Drochia	V-8
Drohobych	IV-4
Drozdovytsia	II-12
Druts, R.	0-10
Druzhba (Zht)	II-8
Druzhba (Chrh)	III-13
Druzhba (Khutir Mykhailivs'kyi)	I-14
Druzhkivka	V-18, Db II-3
Druzhne, Dn	III-4
Druzhne (Vr), Db	III-7
Drzewiczka, R.	II-1
Dubechne	II-5
Dubenka	II-4
Dubets'ko	IV-3
Dubivs'kyi, Dn	III-6
Dubliany	IV-4
Dubno (Dębno) (Pol)	III-3
Dubno (Rv)	III-6
Dubosari	VI-10
Dubove	V-4
Duboviazivka	II-14
Dubovka	IV-25
Dubovskoie	VI-23
Dubovskoie	VIII-23
Dubovychi	II-14
Dubovyky	V-17
Dubrovytsia	II-7
Dubrynych	V-3
Dudchany	VI-14
Dukla	IV-2
Duklia Pass	IV-2
Dulovo	X-8
Dumbrăveni	VII-5
Dumnyi Potik, R.	IV-5
Dunaivtsi	V-7
Dunărea Veche, R.	IX-9
Dunajec, R.	IV-1
Dvorichchia, Dn	II-4
Dvorichna	IV-18
Dvuluchne	III-19
Dykan'ka	IV-15
Dymer	III-11
Dymytrove	V-18; Db III-2

Dymytrove	V-14
Dynivtsi	V-7
Dynów	IV-3
Dytiatky	II-11
Dyviziia	VIII-10
Dyvne	VIII-24
Dyvovka	0-14
Dyvyn	II-5
Dzerzhyns'ke (Romanivka)	III-8
Dzerzhyns'ke	V-18; Db III-3
Dzhankoi	VIII-15
Dzhanybek	IV-27
Dzharylhach Bay	VII-13, 14
Dzharylhach Isl.	VII-13, 14
Dzharylhach, L.	VIII-13
Dzhubha	IX-19
Dzhulynka	V-10
Dzhurak-Sal, R.	VII-24
Dzhuryn	V-9
Dzhuryn	IV-6
Dzhuryn, R.	V-6
Dzialoszyce	III-1
Dziun'kiv	IV-10
Dzvyniach	V-5
Dzyhivka	V-9

E

East European Central Upland	II-16
Eastern Beskyds	IV-2
Eastern Carpathians	IV-2
Edineţi	V-8
Eforie	IX-9
Elanu, R.	VII-9
El'brusskii	X-23
El'buzd, R.	VII-20
Elista	VII-25
El'ton	IV-27
El'ton, L.	IV-27
Enem	IX-19
Enerhodar	VI-15
Engelsove	V-20; Db III-7
Erken-Shakhar	IX-22
Ertil'	II-21
Eskhar	IV-17
Essentuky	IX-23

F

Făgăraş Mts.	VIII-5
Făgăraş	VIII-5
Făget Mts.	VI-4
Făleşti	VI-8
Fălticeni	VI-7
Fărcău, Mt.	VI-5
Fars, R.	IX-21
Fashchivka, Dn	III-5
Fatezh	I-16
Făurei	VIII-8
Fedorivka	V-13
Fedorivka	VI-19
Fedorivs'ka	VIII-19
Fedorovka	V-29
Fedotova Spit	VII-16
Fehérgyarmat	VI-3
Fekete-Körös, R.	VII-2
Feredeu Mts.	VI-6
Feteşti	IX-8
Fieni	VIII-6
Fisht, Mt.	X-20
Floreşti	VI-9
Focşani	VIII-8
Fontanka	VII-11
Foros	IX-14
Frolovo	IV-24

Frunze (Vr)	*V-19; Db II-5*
Frunze (Khrs)	*VII-15*
Frunzens'ke	*IX-15*
Frunzivka (Pl)	*IV-14*
Frunzivka (Zakharivka)	
(Od)	*VI-10*
Furmanovo	*IV-30*

G

Găeşti	*IX-6*
Galaţi	*VIII-9*
Galicia, Hist. Reg.	*IV-4*
Galkin, Isl.	*VIII-29*
Garwolin	*II-2*
Gelnica	*V-1*
General-Toshevo	
(Kasem)	*X-9*
George Estuary	*VIII-9*
Georgievsk	*IX-24*
Gheorghe Gheorghiu-Dej	*VII-7*
Gheorgheni	*VI-6*
Gheorghiu-Dej (Lisky)	*III-20*
Gherla	*VI-4*
Ghidighici	*VI-9*
Ghimeş Pass	*VII-6*
Gigant	*VII-22*
Giraltovce	*IV-2*
Girei	*VIII-21*
Giumalău, Mt.	*VI-6*
Giurgeul Mts.	*VII-6*
Giurgiu	*X-6*
Glavacioc, R.	*IX-6*
Glazunovka	*I-17*
Glodeni	*VI-8*
Głogów Małopolski	*III-2*
Główno	*II-0*
Gmelinka	*III-27*
Golovinka	*X-20*
Góra Kalwaria	*II-2*
Goragorskii	*X-26*
Gorgany, Mts.	*V-4*
Goriachovodskii	*IX-24*
Gor'kaia Balka, R.	*IX-25*
Gor'ko-Solionoie, L.	*IV-27*
Gorkovskii	*V-25*
Gorlice	*IV-2*
Gorlice-Sianik Basin	*IV-2*
Gorniatskii	*V-21*
Gornii	*VI-21; Db IV-8*
Gorodishche (Vlg)	*V-25*
Goronda	*V-3*
Gorshechnoie	*II-19*
Grachevka, R.	*VIII-23*
Granitne	*III-10*
Greaca, L.	*IX-7*
Griazi	*I-20*
Great Caucasus, Mts.	*IX-19*
Great Hungarian Lowland	*IV-2*
Great Tkhach, Mt.	*IX-21*
Grinduş, Mt.	*VII-7*
Grodzisk Mazowiecki	*I-1*
Groza Petru Dr.	*VII-3*
Grofa, Mt.	*V-4*
Grojec	*II-1*
Groznyi	*X-26*
Grybów	*IV-1*
Gubkin	*II-18*
Gudermes	*X-27*
Gul'kevichi	*VIII-21*
Gumrak	*V-25*
(Gundorovka)	*V-21*
Gura Humorului	*VI-6*
Gurghiul Mts.	*VII-6*
Gutîi Mts.	*VI-4*

Gvardiis'ke	*V-16*
Gvardiis'ke	*IV-7*
Gvardiis'ke	*VIII-15*
Gyula	*VII-2*

H

Hadiache	*III-14*
Haichur, R.	*VI-17*
Haidúdorog	*VI-2*
Haidúböszörmény	*VI-2*
Haidúhadház	*VI-2*
Haiduk	*IX-18*
Haidúnánás	*VI-2*
Haiduszoboszló	*VI-2*
Hainivka (Hainówka)	*I-4*
Haisyn	*V-10*
Haivoron	*IV-10*
Haivoron	*V-10*
(Hainówka)	*I-4*
Halych	*IV-5*
Halych, Mt.	*IV-3*
Hamcharka	*VIII-9*
Hannivka, Dn	*III-5*
Hannivka (Mk)	*V-12*
Hantsavychi	*I-7*
Harghita Mts.	*VII-6*
Hariachkivka	*V-9*
Hariachyi Kliuch	*IX-20*
Haspra	*IX-15*
Havrylivka, Db	*I-5*
Havrylivka	*V-17*
Hegyalja, Mt.	*V-2*
Heighland of Kielce-Sandomierz	*II-1*
Heighland of Stavropol	*VIII-22*
Helendzhyk	*IX-19*
Hel'miaziv	*IV-12*
Heniches'ke	*VII-15*
Heniches'ke, L.	*VII-15*
Heorhiivka	*V-20; Db III-6*
Heorhiivs'ka	*IX-23*
Hermakivka	*V-7*
Hermanovychi	*IV-3*
Hernád R.	*V-2*
Hertsa	*V-7*
High Beskyd, Mts.	*V-4*
Hiiche	*III-4*
Hil'tsi	*III-13*
(Hînceşti) Kotovs'ke	*VII-9*
Hirkyi Lim.	*VII-15*
Hîrlău	*VI-7*
Hirne	*V-20; III-7*
Hirne, Dn	*III-4*
Hirnyk	*V-18; Db III-2*
Hirnyk	*III-5*
Hirnyts'ke	*V-15*
Hirnyts'ke	*VI-19; Db IV-5*
Hirsivka	*VII-16*
Hirs'ka Poroda	*VI-20*
Hirs'ke	*V-19; Db II-4*
Hirs'kyi Tikych, R.	*IV-10*
Hîrşova	*IX-8*
Hîrtibaciu, R.	*VIII-5*
Hîrtibaciu Upland	*VIII-5*
Hirzhavka	*VI-9*
Hladkivka	*VII-13*
Hlafyrivka	*VII-19*
Hlevakha	*III-11*
Hlobyne	*IV-14*
Hlodosy	*V-12*
Hlukhiv	*II-14*
Hlukhivtsi	*IV-9*
Hlusha	*0-9*
Hlushkevychi	*II-8*
Hlushkove	*II-15*

Hlusk	*I-9*
Hlyboka	*V-6*
Hlyboka, R.	*V-21; Db II-8*
Hlybokyi, Dn	*II-5*
Hlybokyi (Rs)	*V-21; Db II-8*
Hlybokyi	*VI-23*
Hlyniany	*IV-5*
Hlyns'k	*IV-9*
Hlyns'k	*V-13*
Hlyns'ke	*III-14*
Hnilec, R.	*V-1*
Hnivan'	*IV-9*
Hnizdychiv	*IV-5*
Hnizna, R.	*IV-6*
Hnyla, R. (Bystra)	*V-22*
Hnyla, R. (Zbruch)	*IV-7*
Hnyla Lypa, R.	*IV-5*
Hnyl'che	*IV-5*
Hnylopiat', R.	*III-9*
Hnylyi Tashlyk, R.	*IV-12*
Hnylyi Tikych, R.	*IV-11*
Hnylyi Yelanets', R.	*VI-12*
Hoholeve	*IV-14*
Hoholiv	*III-12*
Hoitkhs'kyi Pass	*IX-20*
Hola Prystan'	*VII-13*
Holhocha	*IV-6*
Hol'mivs'kyi, Dn	*III-4*
Holoby	*I-6*
Holohory Upland	*IV-6*
Holovanivs'ke	*V-11*
Holovchyne	*III-16*
Holovne	*II-5*
Holubivka, Db	*I-4*
Holubivka	*V-16*
Holy Cross Mts.	*III-1*
Holynchyntsi	*V-9*
Homel'	*I-11*
Horbachevo-Mykhailivka, Dn	*IV-4*
Horbuliv	*III-9*
Hordii, Mt.	*V-5*
Horlivka	*V-19; Db III-4*
Hornád, R.	*V-1*
Hornostaipil'	*II-11*
Hornostaivka (Krm)	*VIII-17*
Hornostaivka (Khrs)	*VI-14*
Horobiivka	*IV-10*
Horodenka	*V-6*
Horodets'	*II-7*
Horodkivka (Zht)	*IV-9*
Horodkivka (Vn)	*V-9*
Horodlo	*III-5*
Horodne	*II-7*
Horodnia	*II-12*
Horodnytsia	*III-8*
Horodok (Rv)	*III-7*
Horodok (Lv)	*IV-4*
Horodok (Khm)	*IV-7*
Horodovykovsk (Bashanta)	*VII-22*
Horodyshche (Br)	*I-7*
Horodyshche, Db	*III-5*
Horodyshche (Klm)	*III-8*
Horodyshche (Chrk)	*IV-12*
Horokhiv	*III-5*
Horokhivka	*III-21*
Horokhovatka, R.	*IV-11*
Horokhuvatka	*IV-18*
Horoshyne	*IV-13*
Hortobágy, R.	*VI-2*
Hortobagy, geogr. reg.	*VI-2*
Horynets'	*III-4*
Horyn', R.	*IV-6, I-8*
Hoshcha	*III-7*
Hoshiv	*IV-4*
Hostahaivs'ka	*VIII-18*
Hostomel'	*III-11*

Hostre, Dn	*III-2*
Hoverlia, Mt.	*V-5*
Hovtva	*IV-14*
Hovtva, R.	*IV-14*
Hrabovets'	*III-4*
Hrachivka	*III-18*
Hrachyky R.	*Db III-7*
Hradyz'ke	*IV-14*
Hraivoron	*III-16*
Hraniv	*V-10*
Hrebeniv	*V-4*
Hrebenne	*III-4*
Hrebenyky	*VII-10*
Hrebinka	*III-13*
Hrebinky	*IV-11*
Hrechyntsi	*IV-8*
Hremiach	*I-14*
Hresivs'kyi	*VIII-15*
Hrodivka	*V-18; Db III-2*
Hromivka	*VII-15*
Hromokliia, R.	*VI-13*
Hrubeshiv	*III-4*
Hrun	*III-15*
Hrun', R.	*III-15*
Hrun'-Cherkes, R.	*III-15*
Hrun-'Tashan', R.	*III-15*
Hrushivka, R.	*VI-21; Db IV-8*
Hrushka	*V-8*
Hrushove, Dn	*III-5*
Hrushuvakha	*IV-17; Db I-1*
Hruz'ka, R.	*VI-19*
Hruz'ke	*V-13*
Hruz'ke	*II-14*
Hruz'ko-Lomivka, Dn	*IV-4*
Hruz'ko-Zorians'ke	*Db IV-4*
Hruz'kyi Yelanchyk, R.	*VI-19*
Hryhoriopil'	*VI-10*
Hryhorivka	*IV-12*
Hrymailiv	*IV-7*
Hryneva	*VI-5*
Hryshkivtsi	*IV-9*
Hryshyne	*III-14*
Hrytsiv	*IV-8*
Hryvens'ka	*VIII-19*
Hubivka	*V-13*
Hubynykha	*V-16*
Huchva, R.	*III-4*
Huedin	*VII-4*
Huiva	*III-9*
Huiva, R.	*IV-9*
Hukove	*V-20; Db III-7*
Huliai-Pole	*VI-17*
Humenne	*V-2*
Hundorivs'kyi, Dn	*III-7*
Hurivka	*V-14*
Hurzuf	*IX-15*
Husarivka, Dn	*II-2*
Husarivka	*IV-17*
Husarka	*VI-17*
Huşi	*VII-9*
Husiatyn	*IV-7*
Hutsul' Alps, Mts.	*V-5*
Hutsul' Beskyd, Mts.	*V-5*
Huty	*III-16*
Hvizdets'	*V-6*

I

Ialomiţa, R.	*VIII-6, IX-8*
Iaşi	*VI-8*
(Ichky)	*VIII-15*
Ichnia	*III-13*
Idokopas, C.	*IX-19*
Ihnatpil'	*II-9*
Ihrovytsia	*IV-6*

Ikel', R.   VI-9
Iki-Burul   VIII-25
Ikopot', R.   IV-7
Ikorets, R.   II-20
Ikva (Boh), R.   IV-8
Ikva (Styr), R.   III-6
Ilarionove   V-16
Ilek, R.   III-16
Illia, R.   II-10
Illichivs'ke   VII-11
Il'inka   VII-20
Il'inka   V-22
Il'inkaia   VII-28
Illinka   V18; Db III-2
Illintsi   IV-10
Ilovais'ke   VI-19; Db IV-4
Ilovlia   IV-25
Ilovlia, R.   IV-25
Il's'kyi   IX-19
Iłża   II-2
Iłżanka, R.   II-2
Ináu, Mt.   VI-5
Ineu   VII-2
Indol, R.   VIII-15
Inhul, R.   V-13, VI-13
Inhulets'   VI-14
Inhulets', R.   V-13, VII-13
Inhulo-Kamianka   V-13
Inozemtsevo   IX-24
Întorsura Buzăului   VIII-7
Ipa, R.   I-10
Ipatovo   VIII-23
Iputs', R.   0-13, I-12
Irdyn'   IV-12
Irgakly   IX-25
Irkliiv   IV-13
Irkliivs'ka   VIII-20
Irpin'   III-11
Irpin', R.   III-10, III-11
Irsha, R.   III-9
Irshans'ke   III-9
Irshava   V-4
Irshava, R.   V-3
Isaiky   IV-11
Isakcha   VIII-9
Ishnovets', R.   VI-9
Ishun'   VIII-14
Iskrivka (Pl)   IV-16
Iskrivka (Krv)   V-14
Iskustvennyi, Isl.   VIII-28
(Islam-Terek) Kirovs'ke
  VIII-16
Ispas   V-6
Isperikh   X-7
Ivaitenky   I-14
Ivana-Franka
(Nahuievychi)   IV-4
Ivane-Puste   V-7
Ivanhorod (Chrh)   II-13
Ivanhorod (Chrk)   V-10
Ivanhorod (Krv)   V-13
Ivaniv   IV-9
Ivanivka, Dn   III-7
Ivanivka (Zht)   III-10
Ivanivka (Kv)   IV-11
Ivanivka (Chrk)   V-11
Ivanivka (Krv)   V-13
Ivanivka   V-19; Db III-5
Ivanivka (Mk)   VI-12
Ivanivka (Od)   VII-11
Ivanivka (Khrs)   VII-15
Ivanivs'ka   VIII-19
Ivankiv   III-10
Ivankivtsi (Khm)   IV-7
Ivankivtsi (Krv)   V-13
Ivano-Frankivs'ke
(Stanyslaviv)   V-5
Ivano-Frankove (Yaniv)   IV-4

Ivanopil' (Yanushpil')   IV-9
Ivanopillia, Dn   III-3
Ivano-Shamsheve   VII-20
Ivanove   I-6
Ivanychi   III-5
Ivanytsia   III-13
Ivatsevychi   I-6
Ivcha   IV-9
Ivers'ke, Db   II-1
Ivkivtsi   III-13
Ivnia   II-17
Ivnytsia   III-10
Iwonicz-Zdrój   IV-2
Ivotka, R.   II-14
Iza   V-4
Iza, R.   VI-5
Iziaslav   III-7
Izium   IV-18; Db I-2
Iziumets', R.   DbI-2
Izmail   VIII-9
Izmalkovo   I-18
Izobil'nyi   VIII-22
Izvaryne   V-20; Db III-7

J

Janów Lubelski   III-3
Janiv (Janów Podlaski)   I-4
(Janów Podlaski)   I-4
Jarosław   III-3
Jasiolka, R.   IV-2
Jasło   IV-2
Jedlicze   IV-2
Jędrzejów   III-1
Jibou   VI-4
Jijia, R.   VI-7
Józefów   I-2
(Juzivka)   V-18

K

Kabannie   IV-19; Db I-4
Kabardynka   IX-18
Kacha   IX-14
Kacha, R.   IX-14
Kachalivka   III-16
Kachanivka   III-13
Kachkarivka   VI-14
Kachyka   VI-6
(Kadiivka)   V-19; Db II-5
Kadyivtsi   V-7
Kagal'nik, R.   VI-22 (Don)
Kahal'nyk, R.
  VII-20 (Sea of Azov)
Kahal'nytskaia   VII-21
Kaharlyk   IV-11
Kahul, L.   VIII-9
Kahul, R.   VIII-9
Kaiasula   IX-26
Kainar, R.   V-8
Kaiukivka, Dn   II-8
Kakhivka Res.   VI-15
Kakhivka   VII-14
Kalach   III-21
Kalach Upland   III-22
Kalach-na-Donu   V-24
Kalaly, R.   VIII-22
Kalamits'ka Bay   VIII-14
Kalanchak   VII-14
Kalarash (Călăraşi)   VI-9
Kalaus, R.   IX-23
Kal'chyk, R.   VI-18
Kaleberdians'kyi
Omel'nyk, R.   V-14
Kalinine   VIII-19
Kalinine   VI-14

Kalinins'k   V-8
Kalinins'ka
(Popovychivs'ka)   VIII-19
Kalinins'ke   VI-13
Kalinins'kyi, Dn   III-7
Kalinkavichy   I-10
Kalius   V-8
Kalius, R.   V-8
Kalmiius, R.   VI-18; Db IV-3
Kalmykivka   IV-19; Db I-5
Kalnybolotskaia   VII-21
Kal'nyk   IV-10
Kal'nykiv   IV-4
Kaluha   VI-13
Kalush   IV-5
Kaluszyn   I-2
Kaluz'ka   IX-19
Kalynivka, Dn   III-4
Kalynivka (Kv)   III-11
Kalynivka (Vn)   IV-9
Kalynivka (Mk)   VI-13
Kalynove, Dn   II-5
Kalyta   III-12
Kalytva, Mt.   V-15
Kalytva, R.   IV-21, V-21
Kamaryn   II-11
Kamennomostskii   IX-21
Kamenolomni
  VI-21; Db IV-8
Kamensk-Shakhtinskii
  V-21; Db III-8
Kamiane   VI-16
Kamiane, Dn   III-6
Kamianets'   I-4
Kamianets'-Podil's'kyi   V-7
Kamiani Mohyly, Nat.
Res.   VI-18
Kamiani Potoky   V-14
Kamianka (Sm)   I-14
Kamianka, Dn   III-6
Kamianka (Vrn)   III-20
Kamianka (Chrk)   IV-13
Kamianka (Khrk)
  IV-18; Db I-2
Kamianka (Vr)   IV-20
Kamianka (Chrv)   V-6
Kamianka (Mol)   V-9
Kamianka (Dnp)   VI-14
Kamianka (Mk)   VII-12
Kamianka, R. (Bazavluk)
  V-14
Kamianka, R. (Vovcha)
  V-17
Kamianka, R. (Dniester) V-9
Kamianka, R. (Ingul)   V-13
Kamianka, R. (Prut)   VI-8
Kamianka, R. (Ros')   IV-10
Kamianka, R. (Uzh)   II-9
Kamianka-Buz'ka
(Kamianka-Strumylivs'ka)
  III-5
Kamianka-Dniprovs'ka
  VI-15
(Kamianka-Strumylivs'ka)
  III-5
Kamians'ke (Zp)   VI-16
Kamians'ke (Od)   VIII-10
(Kamians'ke)
Dniprodzerzhyns'ke   V-15
Kamianyi Brid (Krv)   V-11
Kamianyi Brid (Zht)   III-8
Kamianyi Mist   V-12
Kamienna, R.   II-1
Kamin' (Br)   I-7
Kamin' (Sm)   II-14
Kamin'-Koshyrs'kyi   II-5
Kamula, Mt.   IV-5
Kamyshin   III-26

Kamyziak   VII-29
Kanava Osmol's'ka, R.   II-9
Kańczuga   IV-3
Kanelivs'ka   VII-20
Kaniv   IV-12
Kanivs'ka   VII-19
Kanizh   V-12
Kantemyrivka   IV-20
Kapatkevichy   I-9
Kapitanivka   V-12
Kapustiany   V-10
Kapustin Yar   V-26
Kapustyntsi   III-15
Karabulak   X-25
Kara-Dag, Mt.   IX-16
Kara-Sal, R.   VI-24
Karachaievsk (Makoian-
Shakhar)   X-22
Karachan, R.   II-22
Karachev   0-15
Karaiets', R.   V-8
Karan', R.   III-12
(Karan') Andriivka   VI-18
Karapchiv   V-6
Karapyshi   IV-11
(Karasu-Bazar)
Bilohirs'ke   VIII-15
Karasyn   II-7
Karatul', R.   III-12
Karatysh, R.   VI-18
Karavan   IV-16
Karczew   I-2
Karierne   VI-14
Karkinits'ka Bay   VIII-13
Karlivka   IV-16
Karl Liebknecht   II-16
Karlo-Libknekhtivs'ke
  V-19; Db II-4
Karlo-Marxove
  V-19; Db III-4
Karma   0-11
Karnaukhivka   V-15
Karpenkove   III-20
Karpivka   VI-20; Db IV-7
Karpylivka   III-11
Kartsan, R.   I-22
(Kasem) General-
Toshevo   X-9
Kashlahach, R.   VI-17;
  Db IV-2
Kaspiiskii   VII-28
Kastornoie   II-19
Kastsiukovka   I-11
Katerynivka, Dn   IV-2
Katerynivka (Rs)   VI-19
Katerynivs'ka   VII-20
(Katerynodar)
Krasnodar   VIII-19
Katerynopil'
(Katerynoslav)
Dnipropetrovs'ke   V-16
Katiuzhanka   III-11
Katlabukh, L.   VIII-9
Katsmaziv   V-8
Kavalierka, R.   VII-20
Kavkaz   VIII-17
Kavkazkaia   VIII-21
Kazanka   VI-13
Kazanskaia   IV-22
Kazantyp, C.   VIII-16
Kazantyp Bay   VIII-16
Kazhulak   VIII-24
Kazennyi Torets', R.
  V-18; Db II-2
Kazimierz   II-2
Kazimierza Wielka   III-1
Kazinka   I-20
Kaztalovka   IV-29

Kazynka (Vrn) III-21
Kazynka (St) IX-23
Kegul'ta VII-25
Kehychivka IV-16
Keke-Usun, L. VIII-26
Keleberda V-14
Kelermeskaia IX-21
Kel'mentsi V-7
Kenzhe X-24
Keramik, Dn III-3
Kerch VIII-17
Kerch Pen. VIII-16
Kerch Strait VIII-17
Kerepets', R. V-3
Kersha, R. 0-22
Ketrysanivka VI-13
Kevsala VIII-23
Kežmarok IV-1
Khabez IX-22
Khabl', R. IX-19
Khadyzhens'ke IX-20
Khadzhybei Lim. VII-11
Khadzhyder, R. VII-10
Khalturine IV-16
Khamturka, R. VI-25
Khans'ke, L. VII-19
Kharabali VI-28
Kharkiv III-17
Kharkiv, R. III-17
Khartsyz'ke V-19; Db III-4
Khasania X-24
Khasaviurt X-27
Khashchuvate V-10
Khava, R. II-20
Khazhyn IV-9
Kherson VII-13
Khersones, C. IX-14
Khlevnoie I-20
Khlibodarivka VI-18
Khliborobnyi VII-21
Khlivchany III-4
Khmelina, R. I-22
Khmeliv III-14
Khmel'nyts'kyi
(Proskuriv) IV-7
Khmel'ove V-12
Khmil'nyk IV-8
Khodoriv IV-5
Khodz', R. IX-21
Khoiniki II-10
Khokhol'skii II-19
Kholm (Chelm) II-4
Kholm Region, hist. reg.
III-4
Kholm Upland II-4
Kholms'kyi IX-19
Kholmy II-13
Khomora, R. IV-8
Khoms'k I-6
Khomulove VI-19
Khomutovka II-15
Khomutovs'kyi Res. VI-19
Khop'or, R. II-22, IV-23
Khorly VII-13
Khorobychi I-12
Khorol IV-14
Khorol, R. III-14
Khorosheve IV-17
Khorostkiv IV-6
Khoruzhivka III-14
Khotiivka I-13
Khotimlia, R. III-18
Khotin' II-15
Khotmyz'k III-16
Khots'kyi Horb, Mt. IV-12
Khotyn (Rv) III-6
Khotyn (Chrv) V-7
Khotyn Upland V-6

Khotynets' 0-16
Khotynychi I-7
Khrapun' II-8
Khreshchatyk V-6
Khrestyshche V-18; Db II-2
Khrestyteleve IV-13
Khrystoforivka (Mk) VI-13
Khrystoforivka (Dnp) VI-14
Khrystynivka V-10
Khukhra III-15
Khust V-4
(Khutir Mykhailivs'kyi)
Druzhba I-14
Khutirs'kyi VII-23
(Khutorok)
Novokubans'k VIII-22
Khvastiv III-10
Khvastivtsi II-13
Khvorostan', R. II-20
Khyl'kivka IV-14
Khyriv IV-3
Kiafar, R. X-22
Kiblych V-10
Kielce III-1
Kiev (Kyiv) III-11
Kiev Plateau III-11
Kiev Res. III-11
Kievan Polissia II-10
Kiliia VIII-10
Kiliia Estuary VIII-10
Kiliia Stara (Chilia-
Veche) VIII-10
Kiltychchia, R. VII-17
Kimchin Lim. VII-26
Kinburn Spit VII-12
Kins'ki Rozdory VI-17
Kinzhal, Mt. X-23
Kipti II-12
Kirgizh, R. VII-10
Kirgizh-Kytai, R. VII-10
Kirove II-10
Kirove V-18; Db III-3
Kirove VI-16
Kirovohrad
(Yelysavethrad) V-13
Kirovs'ke IV-18; Db I-3
Kirovs'ke (Dnp) V-15
Kirovs'ke V-19; Db II-5
Kirovs'ke V-19; Db III-4
Kirovs'ke (Islam-Terek)
VIII-16
Kirovskii VIII-29
Kirpili Lim. VIII-19
Kirpili, R. VIII-19
(Kishinev) VI-9
Kislovodsk X-23
Kisvárda V-3
Kitsman' V-6
Kivshuvata IV-11
Kiziliurt X-27
Kizliar X 27
Kizliar Bay IX-27
Klavdiievo-Tarasove III-11
Kleban' V-10
Kleban'-Byk, R. V-18
Kleban'-Byk Res. V-18;
Db III-3
Klembivka V-9
Klenovyi V-20; Db III-6
Klesiv II-7
Kletskii IV-24
Klevan' III-6
Kleven', R. II-15
Klintsy I-13
Klishkivtsi V-7
Klodnytsia, R. IV-4
Klymovo I-13
Klyntsi V-13

Klyshky II-14
Kobeliaky IV-15
Kobolchyn V-8
Kobryn' I-5
Kobyzhcha III-12
Kocheriv III-10
Kocherizhky V-16
Kochetok IV-17
Kochetovka I-21
Kochety, R. VIII-20
Kock II-3
Kodema, Dn II-4
Koden' II-4
Kodnia III-9
Kodra III-10
Kodry Upland VI-9
Kodyma V-10
Kodyma, R. V-10
Kohyl'nyk (Kunduk), R.
VII-9
Kojsovs'ka Hola, Mt. V-1
Kokorevka I-15
Koksovyi V-21
Kolbuszowa III-2
Koliadivka IV-20
Kolisne VII-10
Kolky (Vl) II-6
Kolky (Rv) II-7
Kolochava V-4
Kolodiaznyi, Dn II-8
Kolodizhne III-20
Kolodne II-7
Kolomak IV-16
Kolomak, R. IV-16
Kolomyia V-6
Kolontaiv IV-15
Kolpny I-18
Kolushkyne V-21
Koluszki II-0
Kolybelka III-20
Komancha IV-3
Komar VI-17
Komariv III-4
Komarivka, Db I-2
Komarivka (Chrh) II-13
Komarivka (Khrk) IV-17
Komarne IV-4
Komarychi I-15
Kominternivs'ke VII-11
Komisarivka, Dn III-5
Komisarivka, Dn III-8
Kompaniivka V-13
Komsomol'ske
(Makhnivka) IV-9
Komsomol'ske (Pl) IV-14
Komsomol'ske (Khrk) IV-17
Komsomol'ske
VI-19; Db IV-4
Komsomol's'kyi, Dn III-7
Komsomol's'kyi, Dn IV-2
Komsomol'skii (Kal) VIII-27
Komsomol'skii (Dag) IX-27
Komunars'ke (Alchevs'ke)
V-19; Db III-5
Komyshany VII-13
Komysheva Bukhta IX-14
Komyshiv VII-23
Komyshna, R. V-20
Komyshne, Dn II-7
Komyshnia III-14
Komyshuvats'ka VII-18
Komyshuvakha
V-18; Db II-2
Komyshuvakha (Vr)
Db II-4
Komyshuvakha (Zp) VI-16
Komysh-Zoria VI-17
Konetspil' V-11

Koniukhy IV-6
Konka (Kins'ka), R. VI-17
Konopel'ka, R. III-6
Konotip II-14
Kóńskie II-1
Konstantinovskii VI-22
(Konstantynów)
Kostiantyniv I-4
Kontarne, Dn III-4
Konyshevka II-16
Kopachanka, R. VI-8
Kopaihorod V-8
Kopani VI-16
Kopychyntsi IV-6
Kopystyryn V-9
Korchivka III-4
Korchyk, R. III-8
Korchyn III-5
Kordelivka IV-9
Kordyshivka IV-9
Koreiz IX-15
Koreneve II-15
Korenivs'k VIII-20
Korets' III-8
Korin', R. III-17
Koriukivka II-13
Korma, L. II-9
Kormove VII-24
Kormyn, R. II-6
Kornyn III-10
Korocha III-18
Korocha, R. III-18
Koroleve V-4
Korop I-13
Koropets' V-6
Koropets', R. V-6
Korosten' III-9
Korostyshiv III-10
Korotych IV-17
Korovyntsi III-14
Korsak, R. VII-16
Korshiv V-6
Korsun', Dn III-4
Korsun'-Shevchenkivs'kyi
IV-12
Kortelisy II-5
Korytna IV-10
Koryzh II-15
Kosava I-6
Koshary IV-22
Koshekhabl' IX-21
Koshkivka, R. VI-11
Košice V-2
Košice-Prešov Basin VII-2
Kosiv V-6
Kosivs'ka, R. V-5
Kosmach V-5
Kostiantyniv (Konstantnów)
I-4
Kostiantynivka, Dn IV-2
Kostiantynivka V-18; Db II-3
Kostiantynivka (Khrk) IV-16
Kostiantynivka (Mk) VI-12
Kostiantynivka (Zp) VII-16
(Kostiantynohrad)
Krasnohrad IV-16
Kostopil' III-7
Kostryzhivka V-6
Kosylove III-16
Kotel'nikovo VI-24
Kotel'va III-15
Kotovka IV-15
Kotovo III-25
Kotovsk I-22
Kotovsk (Hînceşti) VII-9
Kotovs'ke (Birzula) VI-10
Kotsiubyns'ke (Berkovets')
III-11

Kovalivka

Kovalivka (Pl) III-15
Kovalivka (Mk) VI-12
Kovel' II-5
Koviahy IV-16
Kovpyta II-11
Kovrai, R. IV-12
Kovsiuh, R. V-20
Kozacha Lopan' III-17
Kozary III-12
Kozats'ke VII-14
Kozelets' III-12
Kozel'shchyna IV-14
Kozhan-Horodok I-8
Kozhanka IV-10
Kozhany I-12
Kozhukhiv IV-8
Kozhukhivka III-11
Koziatyn IV-9
Kozienice II-2
Kozliv IV-6
Kozlivka III-21
(Kozlov) Michurins'k I-21
Kozova IV-6
Kozyn (Rv) III-6
Kozyn (Kv) III-11
Kozyn (Kv) IV-12
Kraina Poliana IV-2
Krakovets' IV-4
Kral'ovsky Chlmec V-2
Kramarivka IV-18
Kramators'ke V-18; Db III-3
Krampna IV-2
Krapynets', R. X-7
Krasenivka IV-13
(Krasiczyn) IV-3
Krasivaia Mecha, R. 0-19
Krasna IV-2
Krasna, R. (Dinets) IV-19; Db I-4
Krasna, R. (Dnieper) III-11
Krasna, Mt. V-4
Krasna Hora 0-12
Krasna Hora, Dn II-4
Krasna Poliana (Dnts) VI-18
Krasnaia Poliana (Krd) X-21
Krasna Poliana (Rs) VII-22
Krasna Slabada I-8
Krasna Yaruha III-16
Krasne, Dn III-2
Krasne (Brn) 0-14
Krasne (Blg) III-19
Krasne (Lv) IV-5
Krasne (Tr) IV-7
Krasne (Vn) V-9
Krasne (Od) VII-10
Krasne (Khrk) VII-13
Krasne (Krd) VII-20
Krasne, L. VII-14
Krasnen'ke VI-10
Krasni Barykady VII-28
Kraśnik III-3
Kraśnik Fabryczny III-3
Krasni Okny VI-10
Krasnoarmeis'kyi VI-23
Krasnoarmiis'ka (Poltavs'ka) VIII-19
Krasnoarmiis'ke (Hryshyne) V-18; Db III-2
Krasnoarmiis'ke VI-18
Krasnodar (Katerynodar) VIII-19
Krasnodars'kyi V-20
Krasnodon (Sorokyne) V-20; Db III-7
Krasnoflots'ke III-22
Krasnogvardeiskoie (Blh) III-19

Krasnogvardiis'ke (Kurman-Kamelski) VIII-15
Krasnogvardiis'kyi (Mykolaivs'ka) VIII-20
Krasnogvardiiskoie (St) VIII-22
Krasnohirka VII-10
Krasnohorivka V-18; Db III-3
Krasnohrad (Kostiantynohrad) IV-16
Krasnoiars'ke VIII-14
Krasnoie I-19
Krasnoïl's'ke V-6
Krasnokuts'ke III-16
Krasnolesnyi II-20
Krasnopavlivka IV-17
Krasnoperekops'ke VIII-14
Krasnopil' IV-9
Krasnopilka V-10
Krasnopillia III-16
Krasnopushcha IV-5
Krasnoselivka IX-15
Krasnosilka (Krv) V-12
Krasnosilka (Od) VII-11
Krasnosillia (Chrk) IV-13
Krasnosillia (Krv) V-13
Krasnoslobodsk V-25
Krasnostav (Khm) III-8
Krasnotorka V-18; Db II-2
Krasnoznamianka Can. VII-13
Krasnyi Kut, Dn
Krasnyi Luch V-19; Db III-5
Krasnyi Lyman V-18; Db II-3
Krasnyi Manych VII-22
Krasnyi Oktiabr, Db III-4
Krasnyi Oktiabr V-19; Db III-4
Krasnyi Profintern V-19; Db III-4
Krasnyi Sulin VI-21; Db IV-8
Krasnyi Yar VII-29
Krasnystav (Krasnostav) III-4
Krasyshyn (Krasiczyn) IV-3
Krasyliv IV-7
Krasylivka II-10
Krasylivka II-12
Kraszna, R. V-3
Krekhaiv III-11
Krekhiv III-4
Kremenchuk Res. IV-13
Kremenchuk IV-14
Kremenivka VI-18
(Kremhes) IV-14
Kremianets' Hills III-6
Kremianets' III-6
Kreminna IV-19; Db I-4
Kripka, R. VI-20; Db IV-6
Kriukove, Dn IV-6
Kriusha, R. IV-23
Krolevets' II-14
Kroma, R. I-16
Krompachy V-1
Kromy I-16
Kropotkin VIII-21
Kropyvnia III-9
Kropyvnia, R. IV-13
Krościenko IV-1
Kroshnia III-9
Krosno IV-2
Kruchena Balka VII-22
Kruhliv VI-6
Krul'man, R. VI-16
Krupets' II-15
Krupoderyntsi IV-13
Kruty II-13

Krychunove VI-11
Kryha, R. II-15
Kryliv III-5
Krylivs'ka VII-20
Krymky V-12
Krymne II-5
Kryms'ke IX-18
Krynka V-19
Krynka, R. VI-19; Db IV-5
Krynychky V-15
Krynychna, Dn III-4
Krynychuvatka V-13
Krynytsia (Br) I-5
Krynytsia (Pol) (Krystynopil') IV-1
Chervonohrad III-5
Kryva Ruda, R. IV-13
Kryva Spit VI-19
Kryvche V-7
Kryve Ozero VI-11
Kryvonosove IV-20
Kryvorivnia V-5
Kryvorizhzhia (Rs) V-21
Kryvorizhzhia, Dn III-1
Kryvyi Rih VI-14
Kryvyi Torets', R. V-18; Db II-3
Kryzhopil' V-9
Krzna, R. I-4
Kshen', R. II-18
Kshenskii II-18
Księżpol III-3
Kuban' Lowland VIII-20
Kuban', R. X-23; VIII-18
Kuban' Res. IX-23
Kubanka VII-11
Kubans'ka IX-20
Kublych, R. V-10
Kubolta, R. V-8
Kubrat X-7
Kucha V-8
Kuchurhan VII-10
Kuchurhan, R. VI-10
Kuchurhan Lim. VII-10
Kuhei VII-20
Kuhoieis'ka VII-21
Kuho-Yeia, R. VII-20
Kuial'nyk Lim. VII-11
Kuibysheve (Zp) VI-17
Kuibysheve VI-18
Kuibysheve (Rs) VI-19; Db IV-5
Kuibysheve (Krm) IX-14
Kuibyshevka VI-12
Kuk, Mt. V-4
Kukhits'ka Volia II-6
Kula, R. VI-9
Kulachkivtsi V-6
Kulak, R. X-7
Kul'baky II-15
Kul'chyny IV-7
Kuleshivka VI-20
Kulykiv IV-5
Kulykivka II-12
Kulykivs'kyi VII-20
Kulynychi IV-17
Kuma, R. X-23
Kuma-Manych Can. VIII-25
Kuma-Manych Depression VI-21
Kumachove, Dn IV-4
Kumshak, R. VI-22
Kumylga, R. III-23
Kumylzhenskaia IV-23
Kundriucha, R. VI-21; Db IV-7
Kundriuchyns'kyi VII-23
Kun'ie IV-18

Kuniv III-7
Kupianka IV-18
Kupianka-Vuzlova IV-18
Kupievakha III-16
Kupil' IV-7
Kura, R. IX-25
Kurakhiv Res. Db. IV-2
Kurakhivka V-18; Db III-2
Kurakhove VI-18; Db IV-2
Kurchans'ka VIII-18
Kurchans'kyi Lim. VIII-18
Kurdiumivka V-18; Db III-3
Kurdzhinovo X-21
Kurdzhyps, R. IX-20
Kurdzynskaia IX-21
Kurganinsk IX-21
Kurhannyi VII-23
Kuriachivka IV-19
Kurkovychi I-13
(Kurman-Kamei'chi) VIII-15
Kursavka IX-23
Kursk II-17
Kurs'ka IX-25
Kurtlak, R. V-23
Kurylivka V-15
Kushchivs'ka VII-20
Kushnytsia V-4
Kushuhum VI-16
Kusnyshcha II-5
Kustivtsi IV-8
Kutais IX-20
Kuteinykivs'ka VI-23
Kuteinykove VI-19; Db IV-4
Kutsivka V-13
Kuty V-6
Kuzemivka IV-18
Kuzhorskaia IX-21
Kuz'myn IV-8
Kvasy V-5
Kyiats'ke L. VIII-14
(Kyiv) III-11
Kyivka VII-23
Kyivs'ke VIII-18
Kyl'chen', R. V-16
Kyrleuts'ke, L. VIII-14
Kyrlybaba VI-6
Kyrykivka III-16
Kyrylivka VII-16
Kyselivka (Khrs) VII-13
Kyselivka (Rs) VI-25
Kyselyn III-5
Kyshen'ky V-15
Kyshyn II-8
Kysliakivs'ka VII-20
Kytai, L. VIII-10
Kytaihorod V-7
Kyvertsi III-6
Kyzyltashs'kyi Lim. VIII-18

L & Ł

Laba, R. IX-21, VIII-20
Labinsk IX-21
Labova IV-1
Lăcăuț, Mt. VIII-7
Łada, R. III-3
Ladan III-13
Ladovskaia Balka VIII-22
Ladoz'ka VIII-20
Ladyzhyn V-10
Ladyzhynka V-11
Lakedemonivka VI-19
Lakhva I-8
Lan', R. I-8
Lanchyn V-5
Łańcut III-3
Lanivtsi IV-7

Lanna	IV-16
Lăpuş, R.	VI-4
Lapuşna, R.	VI-9
Larga, R.	VII-9
Laryne	VI-18; Db IV-3
Lashchiv	III-4
Łaskarzew	II-2
Latnaia	II-19
Lavochne	V-4
Lavriv	III-6
Lavriv	IV-3
Lazarevskoie	X-20
Lazirky	III-13
Lazovs'k (Sîngerei)	VI-9
Lebedian'	0-20
Lebedivka	VIII-11
Lebedyn	III-15
Lebedynka	V-11
Lebiazhyi Lim.	VIII-19
Łeczna	II-3
Left Bank Ukraine	II-12
Łeg, R.	III-2
Legionovo	I-1
(Leipzig) Serpneve	VII-10
Lel'chytsi	II-9
Lenin Can.	X-25
Lenin, L.	V-16
Lenin	I-8
Lenine (Sim Kolodiaziv)	
	VIII-16
Leninhrads'ka (Umans'ka)	
	VII-20
Leninsk	V-26
Lenins'ke	V-20; Db III-7
Lenins'ke, Dn	III-3
Lenins'kyi	VI-9
Lenkivtsi	V-7
Leova	VII-9
Lermontovskii	IX-24
Leshniv	III-6
(Lesko)	IV-3
Les'ky	IV-13
Lesnoi Voronezh, R.	I-21
Lesnoi Tambov, R.	I-22
Letia	VIII-10
Letnaia Stavka	VIII-24
Lev Tolstoi	0-20
Levoča Mts.	IV-1
Levoča	IV-1
Leżajsk	III-3
L'gov	II-16
Liaborets', R.	IV-2
Liadomyrova	IV-2
Liadova, R.	V-8
Liashkivka	IV-15
Liashky	III-3
Liatorytsia, R.	V-4, V-2
Liatychiv	IV-8
Lieliukhiv	IV-1
Likhovskoi	V-21; Db III-8
Liman (As)	VIII-28
Limanowa	IV-1
Limna	IV-3
Limnytsia, R.	V-5
Lipa, R.	I-11
Lipcani	V-7
Lipetsk	I-20
Lipliave	IV-12
Lipova	VII-2
Lipsko	II-2
(Lisivka)	Db III-2
Lisivshchyna	III-9
Liska, R.	IV-24
Lis'ko (Lesko)	IV-3
(Lisky)	III-20
Lisna, R.	I-4
Lisne, Dn	III-4
Litky	III-11

Little Poland Upland	III-1
Little Polissia, geogr. reg.	
	III-6
Lityn	IV-9
Liubachiv (Lubaczów)	III-4
Liubachivka, R.	III-3
Liuban'	I-9
Liubar	IV-8
Liubarka	II-10
Liubartsi	III-12
Liubashivka	VI-11
Liubech	II-11
Liubeshiv	II-6
Liubiaz'	II-6
Liubiazh, L.	II-6
Liuboml'	II-5
Liubopil'	VII-12
Liubotyn	IV-16
Liubytiv	II-5
Liudvyshche	III-6
Liuta	V-3
Liuta, R.	V-3
Liuten'ka	III-15
Liutovys'ka	IV-3
Livadiia	IX-15
Livny	I-18
Livokums'ke	IX-25
Livyi Tuzliv, R.	Db IV-6
Liwiec, R.	I-3
Lobanove	VIII-15
Loev	II-11
Log	IV-24
Lohove	III-17
Lohyshyn	I-7
Lokachi	III-5
Lokhvytsia	III-14
Lokhvytsia, R.	III-13
Lokot'	I-15
Łomazy	II-4
Lomuvatka, Dn	II-5
Loo	X-20
Lopan', R.	III-17
Lopandino	I-15
Lopan'ka	VII-21
Lopatyn	III-5
Loseve	III-21
Losiach	V-7
Łosice	I-3
Losie	IV-2
Loshkarivka	VI-15
Losynivka	III-12
Lotasheve	V-11
Lotykove, Dn	II-5
Low Beskyd	V-4
Lower Don Lowland	VI-21
Łowicz	I-0
Loziys'kyi	V-19; Db II-5
Lozna	IV-9
Lozno-Oleksandrivka	IV-19
Lozova	V-17
Lozova, R. (Murafa)	V-9
Lozova, R.	V-19; Db II-5
Lozovatka, R.	VII-17
Lozove (Khm)	IV-8
Lozove	IV-18; Db I-3
Lozoven'ka	IV-17
Lubartów	II-3
Lublin	II-3
Lublin Upland	II-3
Lubni	III-14
Luchanky	II-9
Luchyna, Mt.	VI-6
Luchynets'	III-9
Ludogorie, geogr. reg.	X-7
Luduş	VII-5
Lugoj	VIII-2
Luh, R.	IV-5
Luha, R.	III-5

Luhanchyk, R.	
	V-20; Db III-6
Luhanka, R.	V-19, II-5
Luhans'ke	V-19; Db III-4
(Luhans'ke)	
Voroshylovhrad	V-20
Luhyny	II-9
Luka, L.	II-4
Lukashivka	VI-15
Lukiv (Matsiiv)	II-5
Lukove, L.	II-5
Łuków	II-3
Lukva, R.	IV-5
Lunachars'ke	VII-17
Lunga, R.	VII-9
Lunka	IX-9
Lunyn	I-7
Lunynets'	I-7
Lupkiv	IV-3
Lupkiv Pass	IV-2
Lutsenkove	III-19
Luts'ke	III-6
Lutuhyne	V-20; Db III-6
Luzhany	V-6
L'va (Mostva), R.	II-8
L'viv	IV-5
Lybokhora	V-3
Lychak, R.	IV-24
Lychkove	IV-16
Lykha, R.	V-21
Lykhachiv	II-12
Lykhivka	V-14
Lyman (Khrk)	IV-17
Lyman (Vr)	IV-19
Lyman (Od)	VIII-10
Lyman, L.	IV-17
Lymanchuk, Dn	III-5
Lymans'ke	VII-10
Lynovytsia	III-13
Lypa, R.	III-5
Lypets'ke	VI-10
Lypne	IV-8
Lypnyky	II-9
Lypova Dolyna	III-14
Lypove	IV-13
Lypovets'	IV-10
Lyptsi	III-17
Lysa Hora	V-12
Lysets' (IF)	V-5
Lysets' (Khm)	V-8
Lyshchychi	I-13
Lyshnivka	II-6
Lysianka	IV-11
Łysica, Mt.	III-1
Lysohir, R.	III-13
Lysohirka	VI-20; Db IV-6
Lysychans'ke	V-19; Db II-4
Lytviaky	III-14
Lytvynivka	IV-20
Lyvenka	III-19

M

Machukhy	IV-15
Măcin	VIII-9
Magura, Mt.	V-4
Mahdalynivka	V-15
Maheriv	III-4
Maiachka	IV-15
Maiachka, R.	Db II-2
Maiaky, Dn	II-3
Maiaky	VII-11
Maidan-Oleksandrivs'kyi	
	V-8
Maikop	IX-21
Maiskii (Rs)	VI-21

Maiskii (K-Bo)	X-25
Makariv	III-10
Makhachkala	XI-28
Makhmud-Mekteb	IX-26
Makiivka, Db	I-3
Makiivka	V-18; Db III-3
Makiivka	III-12
Makiivka	IV-11
(Makoian-Shakhar)	
Karachaivs'k	X-22
Makoshyne	II-13
Makovytsia, Mts.	V-3
Maksym	II-11
Maksymivka, Dn	IV-3
Maksymivka (Tr)	IV-6
Maksymivka (Pl)	IV-16
Maksymovychi	II-10
Mala Bilozerka	VI-15
Mala Danylivka	III-17
Mala Divytsia	III-13
Mala Karasivka, R.	IX-15
Mala Laba, R.	X-21
Mala Lokhnia	I-16
Mala Nekhvoroshcha	IV-15
Mala Tersa, R.	V-16
Mala Vil'shanka	IV-11
Mala Vys', R.	V-12
Mala Vys'ka	V-12
Malaia Kazanka, R.	III-25
Mal'chevs'ka	IV-21
Malgobek	X-25
Maliivka	VI-13
Mali Min'ky	II-10
Malka, R.	X-23
Maloarkhangelsk	I-17
Malokaterynivka	VI-16
Małomykhailivka	V-17
(Małopolska, hist. reg.)	
Little Poland	IV-1
Maloriazantseve	
	V-19; Db II-4
Maloryta	II-5
Malotaranivka, Dn	II-3
Maltsiv	IV-2
Malyi Gashun	VII-24
Malyi Gashun, R.	VI-23
Malyi Katlabukh, R.	VIII-9
Malyi Kuberle, R.	VI-23
Malyi Kuial'nyk, R.	VI-11
Malyi Nesvitai, R.	Db IV-7
Malyi Seret, R.	V-6
Malyi Utliuk, R.	VII-16
Malyi Uzen', R.	IV-29
Malyi Zelenchuk, R.	IX-22
Malyn	III-10
Malynivka, Dn	II-3
Malynivka (Khrk)	IV-17
Malynivka (Mk)	VI-12
Mamaia	IX-9
(Mamaivtsi) Novosilka	V-6
Mamalyha	V-7
Manchenky	IV-16
Mandrove	III-19
Manevychi	II-6
Mangalia	X-9
Maniava	V-5
Manina, R.	III-22
Man'kivka	V-11
Man'kove	IV-21
Manych, R.	VII-24
Manych-Gudilo, L.	VII-23
Mara, R.	VI-4
Mărăşeşti	VIII-8
Mărculeşti	VI-9
Mardarivka	VI-10
Marganets'	VI-15
Marghita	VI-3
Marfivka	VIII-17

Marianivka III-5
Marians'ka VIII-19
Marians'ke VI-14
(Mariiupil') Zhdanov VI-18
Marinka VI-18; Db IV-3
Mar'ivka VI-15
Marki I-2
Markivka IV-20
Markivka, R. V-9
Marky III-20
Marmarosh Basin V-4
Marmarosh-Bukovinian
Mts. V-5
Martynivka IV-12
Marukha, R. X-22
Marynivka (Mk) VI-11
Marynivka (Od) VI-11
Masandra IX-15
Masheve I-13
Mashivka IV-15
Matche III-4
Mátészalka VI-3
Matsesta X-20
(Matsiiv) Lukiv II-5
Matusiv IV-12
Matviiv Kurhan VI-19
Matyra, R. I-21
Mazovia, hist. reg. II-0
Mazovian Lowland I-1
Mechebylove IV-17
Mechetka (Kahalak), R.
VII-21
Mechetka (Bolshaia), R.
V-22
Mechetynskaia VII-21
Medenytsia IV-4
Medgidia IX-9
Mediaş VII-5
Medna II-4
Medvedivka IV-13
Medveditsa, R. III-25, IV-23
Medvedivs'ka VIII-20
Medvenka II-17
Medvezhanka, Dn III-7
Medvyn IV-11
Medyka IV-3
Medzhybizh IV-8
Medzilaborce IV-2
Mehanom, C. IX-16
Meleshkovychi II-9
Melitopil' VII-16
Melnyk I-4
Mel'nytsia II-6
Mel'nytsia, R. II-7
Mel'nytsia-Podil's'ka V-7
Mena II-13
Mena, R. II-13
Menchiv, Mt. IV-1
Menchiv, Mt. V-4
Menchykury VI-15
Merefa IV-17
Merlia, R. III-16
Mertvovod, R. VI-12
Metaliferi Mts. VII-3
Metiolkyne, Dn II-5
Mezenivka III-16
Mezeş Mts. VI-3
Mezhova V-17
Mezhove, Dn IV-4
Mezhyrich IV-12
Mezyn II-14
Mglin 0-13
Miakoty III-7
Michalovce V-2
Michurinsk (Kozlov) I-21
Middle Beskyd IV-3
Middle-Carpathians
Depression IV-3

Międzyrzec Podlaski II-3
Mielec III-2
Miercurea-Ciuc VII-6
Miius, R. VI-19; Db IV-5
Miius Lim. VI-19
Miiusyns'ke V-19; Db III-5
Mikashevichy I-8
Mikhailovka III-24
Mikhailovskaia IX-21
Milanówek I-1
Milashevychi II-8
Milcov, R. VII-8
Miletin, R. VI-7
Miliutyns'ka V-22
Millerove, Dn IV-6
Millerovo (Rs) V-21
Milove IV-21
Miluvatka IV-19
Mineral'nyie Vody IX-24
Mingrel's'ka VIII-19
Mińsk Mazowiecki I-2
Mirchyk, R. III-16
Mishkivs'ka IV-22
Miskolc V-1
Mistky IV-19
Mizhhiria (Volove) V-4
Mizhvodne VIII-13
Miziakiv IX-9
Mizil VIII-7
Mizoch III-7
Mizoch Ridge III-6
Mizunka, R. V-4
Mliiv IV-12
Mlyniv III-6
Mnoha, R. III-13
Mochulianka III-8
Modlin I-1
Modrychi IV-4
Mogielnica II-1
Mohyla-Honcharykha, Mt.
VI-18
Mohyla-Bel'mak Mt. VI-17
Mohyla-Mechetna, Mt.
V-19; Db III-5
Mohyliany VI-17
Mohyliv V-15
Mohyliv-Podil's'kyi V-8
Moineşti VII-7
Mokhra II-6
Mokiivtsi III-8
Mokra Kalyhirka V-12
Mokra Moskovka, R. VI-16
Mokra Sura, R. V-15
Mokra Volnovakha, R.
IV-18; Db IV-3
Mokraia Buivola, R. VIII-24
Mokri Yaly, R. VI-17;
Db IV-1
Mokriany II-5
Mokroielanchyk, Dn IV-5
Mokryi Gashun VII-23
Mokryi Karamyk, R. IX-24
Mokryi Tashlyk, R. IV-12
Mokryi Yelanchyk, R.
VI-19; Db IV-5
Mokvyn III-7
Moldava V-1
Moldova, R. VI-6
Moldovean, Mt. VIII-5
Moldovian Upland VI-7
Moldovian
Subcarpathian VI-7
Moldoviţa, R. VI-6
Molochans'ke VI-16
Molochna, R. VII-16
Molochna L. VII-16
Molodizhne V-13

Molodogvardiis'ke
V-20; Db III-7
Molotkovychi I-6
Monashi VII-11
Monastyrshchyna IV-21
Monastyryshche (Chrh)
III-13
Monastyryshche (Chrk)
V-10
Monastyrys'ka IV-6
Mordovo I-21
Mordy I-3
Moreni IX-6
Morivs'ke II-11
Moroch, R. I-8
Morochne II-6
Morozivka (Vrn) III-20
Morozivka (Vn) IV-10
Morozovsk V-22
Morshyn IV-4
Mors'ke IX-15
Morskoi Biriuchok, Isl. IX-28
Moryntsi IV-12
Moshny IV-12
Mos'panove IV-17
Mospyne VI-19; Db IV-4
Mostiştea, R. IX-7
Mostove VI-11
Mostovskoi IX-21
Mostys'ka IV-4
Motil' I-6
Motovylivka III-11
Motronivka V-14
Motyzhyn III-10
Mozdok X-25
Mozhaivka V-20; Db II-7
Mozh, R. IV-16
Mozyr I-10
Mozyr Ridge I-10
Mroga, R. II-0
Mryholod IV-3
Mszczonów II-1
Mtsensk 0-17
Mukachiv V-3
Mukhavets', R. I-5
Muksha, R. V-7
Mumra VIII-28
Murafa, R. V-8
Murashka, R. V-9
Muratove V-19; Db II-5
Mureş, R. VII-6, VII-2
Murom III-17
Murovani Kurylivtsi V-8
Muszyna IV-1
Muzhyche III-22
Muzhyliv IV-6
Muzykivka VII-13
Myhaï VII-11
Myka, R. III-9
Mykhailivka, Dn III-5
Mykhailivka (Sm) III-15
Mykhailivka (Khm) IV-8
Mykhailivka (Chrk) IV-13
Mykhailivka (Pl) IV-15
Mykhailivka (Vrn) IV-20
Mykhailivka (Dnp) V-16
Mykhailivka (Vr)
V-20; Db III-6
Mykhailivka (Zp) VI-16
Mykhailivka (Od) VIII-10
Mykhailo-Kotsiubyns'ke
(Berkovets') II-12
Mykhailo-Lukasheve VI-16
Mykhailovo-
Oleksandrivs'kyi IV-21
Mykil's'ke, Dn IV-2

Mykolaievo-Kozlovs'kyi
VI-19
Mykolaiv (Mk) VII-12
Mykolaivka, Dn II-3
Mykolaiv (Lv) IV-4
Mykolaiv (Khm) IV-7
Mykolaivka (Khrk) IV-18
Mykolaivka (Dnp) V-15
Mykolaivka (Dnp) V-17
Mykolaivka (Dnts)
V-18; Db II-3
Mykolaivka (Od) VI-11
Mykolaivka (Mk) VI-13
Mykolaivka (Dnp) VI-14
Mykolaivka (Rs) VI-19
Mykolaivka VI-19; Dn IV-4
Mykolaivka Db IV-3
Mykolaivka (Od) VII-11
(Mykolaivs'ka)
Krasnogvardiis'kyi VIII-20
Mykol's'ke III-22
Mykulychyn V-5
Mykulyntsi (Tr) IV-6
Mykulyntsi (Vn) IV-9
Mykytivka III-19
Myloradove IV-15
Myn'kivtsi V-8
Myrhorod IV-14
Myrivka IV-11
Myrna Dolyna, Dn II-4
Myrne, Dn III-7
Myrne (Dnp) V-14
Myrne (Dnts) VI-18
Myrne (Khrs) VII-14
Myrnyi III-9
Myronivka (Kv) IV-11
Myronivka (Krv) V-14
Myronivka (Dnp) VI-15
Myronivs'kyi Db III-4
Myropil' III-8
Myropillia II-16
Myroslavl' III-8
Myrove VI-15
Myshuryn Rih V-14
Myshyn V-5
Mysove VIII-16
Mytiakins'ka V-20; Db II-7
Mytiakynka, R. V-21; Db II-7
Mytky V-8
Mytrofanivka IV-20
Myshkova, R. V-24
Myzove II-5
Mzynta, R. X-21

N

Nadezhda IV-15
Nadlak V-12
Nadterechnaia X-26
Nadtochaivka IV-12
Nadvirna V-5
Naftohors'ke IX-20
Nagykálló VI-2
Nahirne VIII-9
Nahol'no-Tarasivka
V-20; Db III-6
Nahol'na, R. (Miius)
VI-20; Db IV-5
Nahol'na (Velyka), R. V-22
(Nahuievychi) Ivana-
Franka IV-4
Nahuts'ke IX-23
Nal'chik X-24
Nain-Shara, R. VII-24
Nałęczów II-3
Naraiv IV-5
Naraivka, R. IV-5

Narodychi *II-10*
Narol' *III-4*
Narovlia *II-10*
Nartkala (Dokshukino) *X-24*
Narev, R. *I-4*
Narev (Narva), R. *I-4*
Narva *I-4*
Naryn-Khuduk *VIII-27*
Naryshkino *I-16*
Năsăud *VI-5*
Nastashka *IV-11*
Nastasiv *IV-6*
Natukhaivs'ka *IX-18*
Nauchnyi *IX-15*
Naurskaia *X-26*
Navlia, R. *I-16*
Navlia *I-15*
Năvodari *IX-9*
Nazran' *X-25*
Neajlou, R. *IX-6*
Nechaiane *VII-12*
Nedobiitsi *VI-9*
Nedoboivtsi *V-7*
Nedoharky *IV-14*
Nedra, R. *III-12*
Nedryhailiv *III-14*
Neftokumsk *IX-25*
Negreşti *VII-8*
Negreşti-Oaş *VI-4*
Negru, R. *VIII-7*
Nekhaevskii *III-22*
Nekhvoroshcha (VI) *III-5*
Nekhvoroshcha (Pl) *IV-15*
Nekrasovs'ka *VIII-20*
Nelipivka, Dn *III-3*
Nemiia, R. *V-8*
Nemira, Mt. *VII-7*
Nemyriv (Lv) *III-4*
Nemyriv (Vn) *V-9*
Nemyryntsi (Khm) *IV-7*
Nemyryntsi (Khm) *IV-8*
Nerubais'ke *VII-11*
Neruch', R. *I-17*
Nerusa, R. *I-16*
Nesterov (Zhovkva) *III-4*
Nesvich, R. *II-11*
Nevel' *II-6*
Nevinnomyssk *IX-22*
Nevinnomyssk Can. *IX-22*
Nevs'ke, Dn *I-3*
Nezamaivs'ka *VII-21*
Nezhehol', R. *III-18*
Nezlobna *IX-24*
Nezvys'ka *V-6*
Nichlava, R. *V-6*
Nida Basin, geogr. reg. *III-1*
Nida, R. *III-1*
Nidzica, R. *III-1*
Nikolaievsk *III-26*
Nikol'skoie *VI-27*
Nisko *III-3*
Nisporeni *VI-9*
Nizhen *II-12*
Nizhnedevitsk *II-19*
Nizhnii Kisliai *III-21*
Nobel' *II-6*
Nobel', L *II-6*
(Nohais'ke) Prymors'ke *VII-17*
Norino *0-14*
Noryn, R. *II-10*
Noryns'ke *II-9*
Nosivka *III-12*
Nova Astrakhan' *IV-19; Db I-5*
Nova Basan' *III-12*
Nova Borova *III-9*
Nova Chortoryia *III-8*

Nova Dmytrivka (Dn) *II-2*
Nova Haleshchyna *IV-14*
Nova Ivanivka *VIII-10*
Nova Kalytva *III-21*
Nova Kakhivka *VII-14*
Nova Kriusha *III-22*
Nova Maiachka *VII-14*
Nova Odessa *VI-12*
Nova Praha *V-13*
Nova Radcha *II-10*
Nova Rus' *V-17*
Nova Sloboda *II-15*
Nova Ushytsia *V-8*
Novaia Usman' *II-20*
Nova Vodolaha *IV-16*
Nova Vyzhva *II-5*
Nove Misto *IV-3*
Nove Selo (Tr) *IV-7*
Nove Selo (Khm) *IV-7*
Novhorodka *V-13*
Novhorod-Sivers'kyi Polissia, geogr. reg. *I-13*
Novhorod-Sivers'kyi *I-14*
Novhorods'ke *V-18; Db III-3*
Novi Bilokorovychi *II-9*
Novi Sanzhary *IV-15*
Novi Strilyshcha *IV-5*
Novi Terny *V-18; Dn III-2*
Novoaidar *V-20; Db II-6*
Novoaleksandrovsk *VIII-22*
Novoamvrosiivs'ke, Dn *IV-5*
Novoanninskii *II-23*
Novoarkhanhel's'ke *V-11*
Novobatais'ke *VII-20*
Novobeisuz'ka *VIII-20*
Novobila *IV-20*
Novobohdanivka *VI-16*
Novoborove, Db *I-5*
Novoborovytsi, Dn *IV-7*
Novocherkassk *VI-21*
Novochervone *IV-19*
Novodereviankivs'ka *VII-20*
Novodmytriivs'ka *IX-19*
Novodmytrivka *VII-15*
Novodnistrovs'ke *V-8*
Novodonets'ka *VIII-20*
Novodonets'ke *V-18; Db II-2*
Novodruzhes'ke *V-19; Db II-4*
Novoekonomichne *V-18; Db III-2*
Novogroznenskii *X-27*
Novohannivka *V-20; Db III-7*
Novohrad-Volyns'kyi (Zviahel') *III-8*
Novohrodivka *V-18; Db III-2*
Novohryhorivka *V-18; Db II-2*
Novoielysavetivka *VI-11*
Novoivanivka *VI-15*
Novoivanivka, Dn *IV-4*
Novokaterynivka, Dn *IV-4*
Novokhopersk *II-22*
Novokhoperskii *II-22*
Novokryms'ke *IX-18*
Novokubans'k (Khutorok) *VIII-22*
Novokurs'ke *VI-14*
Novokyivka (Mk) *VII-13*
Novokyivka (Khrs) *VII-14*
Novolakskoie *X-27*
Novoleushkivs'ka *VIII-20*
Novomalorosiis'ka *VIII-20*
Novomins'ka *VII-19*
Novomlynivka *VI-17*
Novomoskovs'ke *V-16*
Novomykhailivka, Dn *IV-2*
Novomykhailivka *VI-17*

Novomykhailivs'kyi *IX-19*
Novomykil's'ke, Db *I-4*
Novomykil's'ke *IV-21*
Novomykolaivka, Dn *III-1*
Novomykolaivka *V-18; Db II-2*
Novomykolaivka (Zp) *VI-16*
Novomykolaivka (Zp) *VII-16*
Novomykolaivka (Rs) *VII-20*
Novomykolaivs'ka *VIII-19*
Novomyrhorod *V-12*
Novomyshastivs'ka *VIII-19*
Novookhtyrka, Dn *II-5*
Novooleksandrivka (Blh) *III-19*
Novooleksandrivka (Vr) *V-20;*
Novooleksandrivka (Krm) *VIII-15*
Novooleksiivka (Khrs) *VII-15*
Novooleksiivka (Khrs) *VII-13*
Novoozivs'ke *VI-19*
Novopashkivs'ka *VII-21*
Novopavlivka (Mk) *VI-11*
Novopavlivka (Dnp) *V-17*
Novopavlivs'ka *X-24*
Novopetrykivka, Dn *IV-1*
Novopetrivs'ke *VI-12*
Novopil' *III-9*
Novoplastunivs'ka *VII-20*
Novoplatnyrivs'ka *VII-20*
Novopokrovka (Khrk) *IV-17*
Novopokrovka (Dnp) *V-15*
Novopokrovs'ka *VIII-21*
Novopskov *IV-20*
Novorossiis'ke *IX-18*
Novorozhdestvens'ka *VIII-20*
Novoselivka *IV-18; Db I-3*
Novoselivs'ke *VIII-14*
Novoselydivka, Dn *III-2*
Novoselyshche *IV-6*
Novoselytsia *V-7*
Novosil' *I-18*
Novosilka *IV-6*
Novosilka (Mamaïvtsi) *V-6*
Novosilky *I-5*
Novospasivka, Dn *IV-6*
Novoshakhtinsk *VI-20; Db IV-7*
Novoshcherbynivs'ka *VII-19*
Novoshepelychi *II-11*
Novosvitlivka *V-20; Db III-7*
Novotavriis'kyi *IX-25*
Novotroïts'ke, Dn *III-2*
Novotroïts'ke (Khrs) *VII-15*
Novotroïts'ke (Dnts) *VI-18; Db IV-3*
Novotroïts'ke (Zp) *VII-17*
Novolytarivs'ka *VIII-19*
Novoukrainka (Dnts) *VI-18; Db IV-2*
Novoukrainka (Krv) *V-12*
Novoukrainka (Zp) *VI-17*
Novoukrains'kyi *VIII-21*
Novovasylivka *VII-16*
Novovasylivka *VII-17*
Novovolyns'ke *III-5*
Novovoronezhskii *II-20*
Novovorontsovka *VI-14*
Novozhylivka *VIII-15*
Novozhytomyr *VI-14*
Novozhyvotiv *IV-10*
Novozybkov *I-12*
Novyi Buh *VI-13*
Novyi Bykiv *III-12*

Novyi Karachai *X-22*
Novyi Liublynets *III-4*
Novyi Oskol *III-18*
Novyi Rops'k *I-13*
Novyi Rozdil *IV-5*
Novyi Svit, Dn *IV-4*
Novyi Terek, R. *X-28*
Novyi Vytkiv *III-5*
Novyi Yarychiv *IV-5*
Novyi Yehorlyk *VII-22*
Nowe Miasto *II-1*
Nowy Dwór Mazowiecki *I-1*
Nowy Sącz *IV-1*
Nucet *VII-3*
Nurzec (Nurets'), R. *I-3*
Nyírbátor *VI-3*
Nyíregyháza *VI-2*
Nyirség, geogr. reg. *VI-3*
Nykopil' *VI-15*
Nyzhankovychi *IV-3*
Nyzhnevolzk *VII-28*
Nyzhnia Duvanka *IV-19*
Nyzhnia Krynka *V-19; Db III-4*
Nyzhnia Tersa, R. *V-16*
Nyzhnia Vil'khova *V-20; Db II-7*
Nyzhnie (Brn) *I-13*
Nyzhnie (Vr) *V-19; Db II-5*
Nyzhnii Baskunchak *V-27*
Nyzhnii Bereziv *V-5*
Nyzhnii Chir *V-24*
Nyzhnii Dunavets' *VIII-10*
Nyzhnii Mamon *III-21*
Nyzhnii Nahol'chyk *V-20; Db III-6*
Nyzhniobakans'kyi *IX-18*
Nyzhniohirs'kyi (Salhyr) *VIII-15*
Nyzhniopokrovka, Db *I-5*
Nyzhni Sirohozy *VII-15*
Nyzhni Torhaï *VII-15*
Nyzhniv *V-6*
Nyzy *III-15*

O

Obertyn *V-6*
Obesta, R. *II-15*
Oblivskaia *V-23*
Obodivka *V-10*
Oboian' *II-17*
Obolon' *IV-13*
Obtove *II-14*
Obukhiv *III-11*
Obytochna, R. *VII-17*
Obytochna Bay *VII-16*
Obytochna Spit *VII-17*
Ochakiv *VII-12*
Ocheretuvate (Dnp) *V-15*
Ocheretuvate (Zp) *VII-16*
Ocheretyne *V-18; Db III-3*
Ocna Mureş *VII-4*
Ocniţa *V-8*
Odessa *VII-11*
Odessa Bay *VII-11*
Odobeşti *VIII-8*
Odorheiu Secuiesc *VII-6*
Odrekhova *IV-2*
Ogiński Can. *I-6*
Oituz Pass *VII-7*
Oituz, R. *VII-7*
Oka, R. *I-17, 0-17*
Oka-Don Plain *0-21*
Okhmativ *IV-11*
Okhtyrka *III-15*
Oktiabrskii *VI-24*

Oktiabrs'ke, Dn III-2
Oktiabrs'ke, Dn IV-2
Oktiabrs'ke (Rs) VII-21
Oktiabrs'ke (Krm) VIII-15
Oktiabrs'kyi IX-19
Oktiabrs'kyi III-17
Oktiabrs'kyi VII-20
Ola, R. I-10
Oleksandriia V-14
Oleksandriia III-7
Oleksandrivka (Vrn) III-21
Oleksandrivka (Krv) V-13
Oleksandrivka (Krv) V-14
Oleksandrivka (Dnts)
V-17; Db II-1
Oleksandrivka (Dnts)
V-18; Db II-2
Oleksandrivka (Mk) VI-12
Oleksandrivka
VI-18; Db IV-3
Oleksandrivka (Zp) VII-16
Oleksandrivka (Krd) VII-19
Oleksandrivka (Rs) VII-20
Oleksandrivka (Krm) VIII-15
Oleksandrivs'ke (Vr)
V-20; Db II-6
(Oleksandrivs'ke)
Zaporizhzhia VI-16
Oleksandro-Kalynove, Dn
III-3
Oleksandropil' (Vr) IV-19
Oleksandropil' (Dnp) V-17
Oleksandrynka, Dn IV-3
Oleksiievo-Druzhkivka
V-18; Db II-3
Oleksiievo-Lozovs'ke IV-21
Oleksiivka (Blh) III-19
Oleksiivka, Dn IV-7
Oleksiivka (Khrk) IV-16
Oleksiivka (Khrk) IV-17
Oleksiivka (Vr) IV-19
Oleksiivka (Vr) IV-20; Db I-6
Oleksiivka (Rs)
VI-19; Db IV-5
Olenivka III-4
Olenivka (Zp) VI-16
Olenivka (Dnts)
VI-18; Db IV-3
Olenivka (Krm) VIII-13
(Olenivs'ki Kariery)
Dokuchaievs'ke VI-18;
Db IV-3
Oleshia Sands VII-13, 14
Oleshnia III-15
Oleshytsi III-4
Oles'ko IV-5
Olevs'ke II-8
Ol'hopil' (Vn) V-10
Ol'hopil' (Mk) VI-13
Ol'hynka (Dnts)
VI-18; Db IV-3
Ol'hynka (Krd) IX-19
Ol'hyns'ka VIII-19
Olim, R. II-19
Oliinyky IV-17
Ol'khovatka, Dn III-4
Ol'khovka IV-25
Ol'khovka, R. III-25
Ol'shanytsia IV-11
Olt, R. VII-6, VIII-5
Oltenița IX-7
Oltush II-4
(Ol'viopil') Pervomais'ke
V-11
Olyka III-6
Olyshivka II-12
Omelianivka VIII-15
Omel'nyk IV-14

Omel'nyk, R. V-14
Omul, Mt. VIII-6
Ondava, R. IV-2
Ondava Hills IV-2
Onufriivka V-14
Onut V-7
Opatów III-2
Opatówka, R. III-2
Opillia Upland IV-5
Opir, R. IV-4
Opishnia IV-15
Opoczno II-1
Opole Lubelskie II-2
Oradea VI-2
Oranzherei VIII-28
Orativ IV-10
Orchyk, R. IV-16
Ordyntsi IV-7
Ordzhonikidze (Dnp) VI-15
Ordzhonikidze (Krm) IX-16
Ordzhonikidzevskii X-22
Orel I-17
Orel', R. IV-17, V-15
Orel'ka, R. IV-17
Orepy III-8
Orhei VI-9
Orikhiv VI-16
Orikhivka (Vr) V-20; Db III-6
Orikhivka (Od) VIII-9
Orikhiv Can. II-5
Orikhove, L. II-5
Oril'ka V-17
Orlik, R. 0-16
Orlivka, Db I-5
Orlivka (Chrh) II-12
Orlivka (Chrh) II-13
Orlivka (Sm) II-14
Orlivka (Rs) VII-20
Orlivka (Krm) VIII-14
Orlivka (Krm) IX-14
Orlovs'kyi VII-23
Orlyne IX-14
Orynyn V-7
Orzhiv III-7
Orzhytsia IV-13
Orzhytsia, R. III-13
Osam, R. X-5
Osavulivka V-20; Db III-6
Osered', R. III-21
Osivka III-8
Oskil, R. II-18, IV-18; Db I-2
Oslava, R. IV-3
Osmoloda V-5
Osoivka III-16
Ostapie IV-14
Oster III-11
Oster, R. II-13
Ostky II-8
Ostra VI-6
Ostroh III-7
Ostrohoz'ke III-20
Ostrovians'kyi VII-23
Ostrowiec Świętokrzyski
III-2
Ostrów Lubelski II-3
Ostrozhets' III-6
Osturnia IV-1
Osypenko VII-17
(Osypenko) Berdians'ke
(Zp) VII-17
Otradnaia IX-22
Otrado-Ol'hyns'ke VIII-22
Otwock I-2
Otynia V-5
Ovadne III-5
Ovchynets' 0-13
Ovidiopil' VII-11
Ovruch II-9

Ozaryntsi V-8
Ozdiutychi III-5
Ozera V-14
Ozeriany (Vl) II-5
Ozeriany (Chrh) III-13
Ozeriany (Tr) V-6
Ozerna (Kv) IV-11
Ozerna (Tr) IV-6
Ozerne (Zht) III-9
Ozerne (Od) VIII-9
Ozhenyn III-7
Oziv (Azov) VI-20
Ozivs'ka IX-19
Ozivs'ke VIII-15

P

Pădurea Graiului Mts. VI-3
Pallasovka III-27
Pal'tso 0-15
Pancheve V-12
Panciu VIII-8
Panino II-21
Paniutyne V-17
Pantaivka V-13
Panteleimonivka Db III-3
Papuzhyntsi V-11
Parafiivka III-13
Parashka, Mt. V-4
Paraskoviivka, Dn II-3
Parchew II-3
Pardyna VIII-9
Parkhomenko V-20; Db II-7
Parkhomivka III-16
Parokhons'k I-7
Partyzany VII-15
Parutyne VII-12
Parychy I-10
Pașcani VI-7
Pashkivs'kyi VIII-20
Pasichna V-5
Pasytsely VI-10
Pavlikeni X-6
Pavlivka (Dnts), Dn IV-2
Pavlivka (Rs), Dn IV-7
Pavlivka (Dnp) V-16
Pavlivka (Od) VI-10
Pavlivs'ka VII-20
Pavlohrad V-16
Pavlovs'ke III-21
Pavlysh V-14
Pavoloch IV-10
Pechenihy IV-17
Pechenihy Res. III, IV-17
Pechenizhyn V-5
Pedynka IV-8
Pelahiivka V-19; Db III-5
Pena, R. III-17
Pen'kivka (Vn) IV-9
Pen'kivka (Vn) V-9
Pen'ky IV-8
Penteleu, Mt. VIII-7
Perechyn V-3
Peredil's'ke, Dn II-6
Peredovaia IX-22
Perehins'ke V-5
Pereiaslav-Khmel'nyts'kyi
III-12
Pereiaslavs'ka VIII-20
Pereima V-10
Perekop VII-14
Perekop Bay VII, VIII-14
Perekop Isthmus VII-14
Perekopivka III-14
Perelazy 0-12
Pereleshinskii II-21
Peremoha (Kv) III-12

Peremoha (Vn) IV-9
Peremyshl' (Przemyśl) IV-3
Peremyshl' Foothills IV-3
Peremyshliany IV-5
Perepys I-12
Pereriv I-9
Peresadivka VI-13
Pereshchepyne IV-16
Peresichna III-16
Peresopnytsia III-7
Pereval's'ke V-19; Db III-5
Perevod, R. III-13
Perha II-8
Perha, R. II-8
Perșani Mts. VIII-6
Pershopokrovka VI-15
Pershotravenka V-15
Pershotravens'ke (Zht) III-8
Pershotravens'ke (Dnp)
V-17
Pershotravneve (Zht) II-9
Pershotravneve (Rv) III-7
Pershotravneve (Dnts)
VI-18
Pervoavgustovskii I-16
Pervomais'ke (Ol'viopil')
V-11
Pervomais'ke (Vr)
V-19; Db II-5
Pervomais'ke (Rs) V-22
Pervomais'ke (Mk) VI-13
Pervomais'ke (Rs) VII-24
Pervomais'ke (Krm) VIII-14
Pervomais'kyi (Khrk) IV-17
Pervomais'kyi (Dnts)
VI-19; Db IV-5
Peshkove VI-20
Peskovatka, R. IV-22
Petrashivka IV-8
Petrivka, Db III-3
Petrivka (Vr) V-20; Db II-6
Petrivka (Od) VII-10
Petrivka (Od) VII-11
Petrivka (Khrs) VII-15
Petrivs'ka VIII-18
Petrivs'ke (Chrh) III-12
Petrivs'ke (Khrk)
IV-17; Db I-1
Petrivs'ke V-19; Db III-5
Petrivtsi IV-14
Petroostriv V-12
Petropavlivka III-21
Petropavlivka
(Shakhtars'ke) V-17
Petropavlovs'kaia VIII-21
Petrove V-14
Petrovskoie (Tm) I-21
(Petrovskoie) Svetlograd
VIII-23
Petrov Val III-26
Petrykiv I-9
Petrykivka V-15
Piaseczno I-2
Piastów I-1
Piatigorsk IX-24
Piatka III-9
Piatnyts'ke III-18
Piatra-Neamț VII-7
Piatyhory IV-10
Piatykhatky V-14
Pidbuzh IV-4
Pidhaitsi IV-6
(Pidhiria) Carpathian
Foothills IV-2
Pidhirna III-22
Pidhirne (Vrn) III-20
Pidhirne (Rs) VII-24
Pidhirtsi IV-5

Pidhorens'kyi III-20
Pidhorodna V-11
Pidhorodne V-16
Pidkamin' IV-6
Pidlyssia IV-5
Pidvolochys'ke IV-7
Pidvysoke V-11
Pieniny, Mts. IV-1
Pietros, Mt. VI-5
Pietros, Mt. VI-6
Pietros (Chornohora), Mt.
   V-5
Pilica, R. II-0, II-1
Pilzno IV-2
Pincota VII-2
Pińczów III-1
(Pins'k) I-7
Pip Ivan (Chornohora Mts.)
   V-5
Pishcha II-4
Pishchana V-10
Pishchane IV-12
Pishchani Isl. VII-19
Pishchanka V-9
Pishchanokops'ke VII-22
Pishchanyi Brid V-12
Pishchats II-4
Piskivka III-10
Pisky Rad'kivs'ki, Db I-3
Pisochyn IV-16
Pistynka, R. V-5
Piteşti IX-5
Pivdenne IV-17
Pivdenne Res. VI-14
Piwniczna IV-1
Plakhtiivka VII-10
Planers'ke IX-16
Plastunivs'ka VIII-20
Platnyrivs'ka VIII-20
Platove, Db III-7
Plav, R. II-8
Plavitsa, R. I-21
Plavni VIII-9
Plaziv III-4
Plekhiv IV-13
Pliashivka, R. III-6
Ploieşti IX-6
Plopiş Mts. VI-3
Ploska, R. VII-21
Ploske (Tr) III-6
Ploske (Kv) IV-11
Ploskoie (Lp) I-19
Plot' VI-10
Plotnytsia I-7
Plotyna, Dn II-8
Pluzhne III-7
Plyskiv IV-10
Plysky II-13
Pnivne II-6
Pobida, Dn IV-5
Pobirka V-10
Pobuz'ke V-11
Pochaiv III-6
Pochep I-14
Podillia, hist. reg. IV-7
Podillia III-12
Podkumok, R. X-23
Podlashia, hist. reg. II-4
Podlashian Lowland II-3
Podlashian Polissia II-4
Podolian Upland IV-5
Podolinec IV-1
Podorozhnie III-13
Pohar I-14
Pohoril'tsi I-13
Pohost', L. I-7
Pohrebyshche IV-10
Pohromets' III-18

Pokats', R. I-12
Pokotylivka IV-17
Pokrovka, Dn IV-4
Pokrovs'ka Bahachka IV-14
Pokrovs'ke, Dn II-4
Pokrovs'ke (Dnp) VI-17
Pokrovs'ke (Rs) VI-19
Pokrovs'ke (Mk) VII-12
Pokrovskoie (Or) I-17
Pokrovskoie (St) VIII-22
Pokuttia, hist. reg. V-6
Pokutian Upland V-6
Polcha Upland III-6
Polgár VI-2
Poliakhove IV-7
Poliana V-3
Polianka III-8
Polis'ke II-10
Polis'ke III-7
Polissia Lowland II-6
Polkva, R. IV-7
Pol'noi Voronezh, R. I-21
Polohy VI-17
Polonne III-8
Polonynian Beskyds V-3
Polonina Rivna, Mt. V-3
Pol'ova III-17
Polovynkyne IV-19; Db I-5
Poltava IV-15
Poltavian Plain III-14
Poltavka, Dn III-2
(Poltavs'ka)
Krasnoarmiis'ka VIII-19
Poltva, R. IV-5
Poluzery, R. IV-15
Pomichna V-12
Pomoriany IV-5
Ponezhukai IX-20
Poniativka VII-11
Poniatowa II-3
Poninka III-8
Ponornytsia II-13
Ponurivka I-13
Ponura Lim. VIII-19
Ponura, R. VIII-19
Ponykovytsia III-6
Ponyri I-17
Popadia, Mt. V-4
Popasna V-19; Db II-4
Popasne V-16
Popel'naste V-14
Popil'nia IV-10
Popivka (Sm) II-14
Popivka, Dn III-7
Popivka (Rs) IV-22
Popov VII-21
(Popovychivs'ka)
Kalinins'ka VIII-19
Poprad, R. IV-1
Poputnaia IX-22
Por, R. III-3
Porach V-1
Porohy V-5
Port-Katon VII-19
Portove VIII-14
Porubne V-7
Poshtove IX-14
Potiivka III-9
Potik IV-12
Potudan', R. II-19
Potutory IV-5
Potylych III-4
Povna, R. V-21
Povors'ke II-6
Pozdeivka V-21
Pozhezhyn II-4
Prahova, R. VIII-6
Praskoveia IX-25

Pravoiegorlyk Can. VIII-22
Prechystivka, Dn IV-2
Predeal Pass VIII-6
Preobrazhenka V-16
Preobrazhenne IV-19
Preslav VII-17
Prešov (Priashiv) IV-2
(Priashiv) IV-2
Priadivka V-15
Pricopan Mts. VIII-9
(Prikumsk) Budionovsk
   IX-25
Prikumskii VIII-26
Primorsk IV-26
Prislop Pass VI-5
Pristen' II-17
Probizhna IV-6
Prohnoi V-20; Db II-7
Prokhladnii X-25
Prokhorovka
(Aleksandrovskii) II-17
Prokhory II-13
Proletarsk VII-22
Proletarskoie Res. VII-23
Proletars'ke V-19; Db III-4
Proletars'kyi, Dn III-6
Proletars'kyi (Blh) III-16
Prorva, R. X-28
Prosiana V-17
(Proskuriv)
Khmel'nyts'kyi IV-7
Proszowice III-1
Protoka, R. (Ros') IV-11
Protoka, R. (Kuban') VIII-18
Protopopivka, Db I-1
Provallia, Dn III-7
Pruchnik IV-3
Prudianka III-17
Pruszków I-1
Prut, R. V-5, VIII-9
Pruzhany I-5
Pryberezhne, Dn III-4
Prybuzhany VI-12
Prydorozhna VIII-19
Pryharivka IV-14
Pryiutnoie VII-24
Prykolotne III-18
Pryluka III-13
Prymors'ke (Dnts) VI-18
Prymors'ke (Dnts) VII-18
Prymors'ke (Od) VIII-10
Prymors'ke (Od) VIII-10
Prymors'ke (Nohais'ke)
   VII-17
Prymors'ko-Akhtars'ke
   VII-19
Prymors'kyi VIII-16
Pryntsivka III-18
Pryozers'ke VIII-25
Pryozivs'ka VIII-19
Pryozivs'ke VII-16
Prypiat' Polissia, geogr.
reg. I-7
Prypiat', R. II-5, II-10
Prypiat' Res. I-8
Pryshyb (Mk) VI-13
Pryshyb (Zp) VI-16
Pryvillia IV-19; Db I-4
Pryvil'na VII-19
Pryvil'ne VI-13
Pryvitne IX-15
(Przemyśl) Peremyshl' IV-3
Przeworsk III-3
Przysucha II-1
Pseashko, Mt. X-21
Psebai IX-21
Psekups, R. IX-20

Psezuapse, R. X-20
Pshada, R. IX-19
Pshekha, R. IX-20
Pshysh, R. IX-20
Psiol (Pslo), R. II-17, IV-14
Ptiche VIII-6
Ptsich, R. I-9
Pucioasa VIII-6
Puławy II-2
Pukhivka III-11
Pukhove III-20
Pulemet, L. II-4
Pushkari (Chrh) I-14
Pushkari (Chrh) III-12
Püspökladány VI-2
Pustomyty IV-4
Pustoviitove IV-14
Putna, R. VIII-7
Putyliv, R. V-6
Putyliv VI-6
Putylivka, R. III-6
Putyvel' II-14
Pyliava IV-8
Pyna, R. I-6
Pyns'ke (Pins'k) I-7
Pyriatyn III-13
Pyrohivka II-14
Pyrohivtsi IV-8
Pyrohove IV-9
Pyrohy IV-14
Pysarivka IV-21
Pysarivka V-9
Pys'menne V-16
Pystyn' V-6
Pyvykha, Mt. IV-14

R

Raba, R. III-1
Rădăuţi VI-6
Radchens'ke IV-21
Radekhiv III-5
Radom II-2
Radomka, R. II-2
Radomyshl' (Vl) III-6
Radomyshl' (Zht) III-10
Radomyśl Wielki III-2
Radul' II-11
Radymno IV-3
(Radzivyliv)
Chervonoarmiis'ke III-6
Radzymin I-2
Radzyń Podlaski II-3
Rafalivka II-6
Raguli VIII-24
Raguli, R. VIII-24
Rahachov 0-11
Raihorod V-10
Raihorodka, Dn II-6
Raihorodok (Dnts)
   V-18; Db II-3
Raihorodok (Zht) IV-9
Rai-Oleksandrivka
   V-18; Db II-3
Rais'ke V-18; Db II-2
Rakhiv V-5
Rakhmanivka VI-14
Rakhny-Lisovi V-9
Rakoshyn V-3
Rakovka, R. 0-18
Ramasukha I-14
Ramon' II-20
Rarău, Mt. VI-6
Răşcani VI-8
Rashivka III-14
Rashkiv VI-9
Rasskazovo I-22

Răstoaca, R. — IX-6
Rata, R. — III-4
Ratne — II-5
Rava-Rus'ka — III-4
Rawa Mazowiecka — II-1
Rawka, R. — II-1
Razelm, L. — IX-9
Razgrad — X-7
Rechytsa — I-11
Reghin — VII-5
Rejowiec — II-4
Reia — III-9
Remety — VI-4
Remontne — VII-24
Reni — VIII-9
Reshetnyky — IV-15
Reshetylivka — IV-15
Respublika — VI-18
Ret', R. — II-14
Reut, R. (Seim) — II-16
Reut, R. (Dniester) — IV-8, VI-9
Revna, R. (Snov) — I-13
Revna, R. (Desna) — I-15
Rezina — VI-9
Riazanskaia — IX-20
Richka — V-5
Ridkivtsi — V-7
Ridkodub, Db — I-3
Right-Bank Ukraine — II-10
Rika, R. — V-4
Rîmnic, R. — VIII-8
Rîmnicu Sărat — VIII-8
Ripky — II-12
Rîsnov — VIII-6
Riv, R. — IV-8
Riven'ky (Blh) — IV-19
Riven'ky (Vr) — V-20; Db III-6
Rivna, Mt. — V-3
Rivne (Rv) — III-7
Rivne (Krv) — V-12
Rizdvianii — VII-22
Rocky Caucasus Range, Mts. — IX-21
Rodakove — V-20; Db II-6
Rodionovo-Nesvitais'ke — VI-20; Db IV-7
Rodna Mts. — VI-5
Rodnykivka — V-13
Rodyns'ke — V-18; Db III-2
Rohalyk — V-21
Rohan' — IV-17
Rohatyn — IV-5
Rohiv — I-12
Rohivs'ka — VIII-19
Rohizka — V-10
Rohoziv — III-12
Rohyntsi — III-14
Rokytne (Rv) — II-8
Rokytne (Blh) — III-16
Rokytne (Kv) — IV-11
Roman — VII-7
Roman-Kosh, Mt. — IX-15
Romanivka (Zht) — III-8
Romanivka (Chrh) — V-11
(Romanivka) Dzerzhyns'ke — III-8
(Romanivka) Basarabka — VII-9
Romankivtsi — V-8
Romen — III-14
Romen, R. — III-14
Romodan — III-14
Ropa, R. — IV-2
Ropczyce — III-2
Ros', R. — IV-10, IV-12
Rosava, R. — IV-11
Roshchakhivka — VI-12
Ros'ka, R. — IV-10

Roşiori de Vede — IX-5
Rosshevatka, R. — VIII-21
Rossosh, R. — V-23
Rossoshka, R. — V-25
Rostavytsia, R. — IV-10
Rostov-na-Donu — VI-20
Rotmistrivka — IV-12
Rozaliivka — IV-11
Rozbyshivka — III-14
Rozdil — IV-5
Rozdil'na — VII-11
Rozdolivka — V-17
Rozdol'ne, Dn — IV-4
Rozdol'ne (Ak-Sheïkh) — VIII-14
Rozdory — V-16
Rozhkao — X-21
Rozhniativ — V-5
Rozhniv — V-6
Rozhnivka — III-13
Rozhyshche — III-6
Rozivka — VI-18
Rozkishne, Dn — III-6
Rožňava — V-1
Rožnów Res. — IV-1
Rozsosh — III-20
Rozsosh, R. — III-20
Rozsypne (Rs) — VII-22
Roztochchia Upland — III-3
Rozwadów — III-3
Rozvazhiv — III-10
Rozvil'ne — VII-22
Rozumivka — VI-16
Rubanivka — VI-15
Rubel' — II-8
Rubizhne (Vr) — IV-19; Db I-4
Rubizhne (Khrk) — III-17
Rudivka (Chrh) — III-13
Rudivka (Vr) — IV-19
Rudka — II-6
Rudky — IV-4
Rudne — IV-4
Rudnia — II-9
Rudnik — III-3
Rudno — II-3
Rudnytsia — V-9
Rukav Turunchuk, R. — VII-11
Rumunian Lowlands — X-6
Runivshchyna — IV-15
Rupea — VII-6
Rusanivka — III-14
Rusava, R. — V-9
Ruse — X-6
Rusenski Lom, R. — X-6
Rus'ka Buiilvka — III-21
Rus'ka Moldavytsia — VI-6
Rus'ka Poliana — VI-5
Rus'ka Poliana — IV-12
Rus'ke (Slo) — IV-3
Rus'ke, Dn — IV-5
Rus'ki Tyshky — III-17
Ruskivtsi — V-2
Rus'kova, R. — VI-5
Rus'kova — VI-5
Ruzhany — I-5
Ruzhychna — IV-7
Ruzhyn — IV-10
Rybakivka — VII-12
Rybnyi Sakryl, L. — IV-30
Rybnytsia — VI-10
Rybnytsia, R. (Oka) — I-17
Rybnytsia, R. (Prut) — V-6
Rybotychi — IV-3
Rydomyl' — IV-6
Ryki — II-2
Ryl'sk — II-15
Rymanów — IV-2
Rynhach, R. — V-7

Ryta, R. — II-5
Ryzhanivka — IV-11
Ryzhany — III-9
Ryzhove — V-17
Ryzyne — IV-11
Rządza, R. — I-2
Rzeszów — III-3
Rzhavka, R. — I-11
Rzhyshchiv — IV-12

S

Sabar, R. — IX-7
Sabinov — IV-2
Sablinskoie — IX-24
Saca, Mt. — VII-6
Săcele — VIII-6
Sad — V-16
Sadhora — V-6
Sadovoie — VI-25
Sahuny — III-20
Sajo, R. — V-1
Saka, R. — VII-10
Sakhans'ke — VI-11
Sakhnivshchyna — IV-16
Saksahan' — V-14
Saksahan', R. — V-14
Saky, L. — VIII-14
Saky — VIII-14
Sal, R. — VI-24, VI-22
Sal-Manych Ridge — VI-22
Salhyr, R. — IX-15
Salhyr Res. — IX-15
(Salhyr) Nyzhniohirs'kyi — VIII-15
Salihorsk — I-8
Sal'kove — V-10
Sal'nytsia — IV-9
Salonta — VII-2
Sals'ke — VII-22
Saltykova Divytsia — II-12
Samara, R. — V-17, V-16; Db II-1
Samars'ke — VII-20
Sambek — VI-20; Db IV-7
Sambek, R. — VI-20
Sambir — IV-4
Samhorodok — IV-9
Samhorodok (Kv) — IV-10
Samosh, R. — VI-3
Sampur — I-22
Sandata — VII-22
Sandomierz Basin — III-2
Sandomierz — III-2
(Sanok) Sianik — IV-3
Sarata — VII-10
Sărata, R. (Prut) — VII-9
Sărata, R. (Ialomiţa) — IX-7
Sarata, R. (Sasyk, L.) — VII-10
Saratovs'ka — IX-20
Sarkad — VII-2
Sarmats'ka, R. — VI-19
Sarny (Rv) — II-7
Sarny (Chrk) — V-10
Sárospatak — V-2
Sarpa Lacs — VI-26
Sarpa — VI-26
Sarych, C. — IX-14
Sasiv — IV-5
Sasyk (Kunduk), L. — VIII-10
Sasyk, L. — VIII-14
Sasynivka — III-13
Sataniv — IV-7
Sátoraljaújhely — V-2
Satu Mare — VI-3
Savala, R. — II-22
Săveni — VI-7

Savos'kyi — VII-23
Savran' — V-11
Savranka, R. — V-10
Savur-Mohyla, Mt. Db — IV-4
Savyntsi — IV-18
Sebeş — VIII-4
Sebeş, R. — VIII-4
Sebes-Körös, R. — VII-2
Sebiş — VII-3
Sečovce — V-2
Sedniv — II-12
Sędziszów Małopolski — III-2
Seim, R — II-18, II-13
Seimeny — IX-9
Sekretarka — V-11
Selietyn — VI-6
Sel'nytsia, R. — V-9
Selydove — V-18; Db III-2
Selyshche — IV-9
Semenivka (Chrh) — I-13
Semenivka (Pl) — IV-14
Semenivka (Mk) — VI-12
Semenivka (Zp) — VI-17
Semikarakorskii — VI-21
Semiluki — II-20
Semtsi — I-14
Semybalky — VI-20
Sencha — III-14
Sengileievskoie, L. — VIII-22
Senkevychivka — III-6
Sen'kove — IV-18
Serafimovich (Ust-Medvedetskaia) — IV-23
Serdyte, Dn — III-4
Serednie — V-3
Ser. Chuluk, R. — VI-8
Ser. Kuial'nyk, R. — VI-11
Ser. Yegorlyk, R. — VII-22
Ser. Yehorlyk — VII-21
Seredyna-Buda — I-15
Seret (Siret) — VI-7
Seret, R. (Danube) — V-6, VI-7
Seret, R. (Dniester) — V-6
Sergievka — IX-23
Serhiivka (Vrn) — III-20
Serhiivka (Dnts) — V-17; Db III-1
Serock — I-2
Serpneve (Leipzig) — VII-10
Setraky — IV-21
Sevastopil' — IX-14
Severynivka — IV-8
(Sevliush) Vynohradiv — V-4
Sevsk — I-15
Sfîntu Gheorghe — IX-10
Sfîntu Gheorghe — VIII-6
Sfîntul-Gheorghe, C. — IX-10
Shabel'kivka — V-18; Db II-2
Shabel's'ke — VII-19
Shabla — X-9
Shablykino — I-16
Shabo — VII-11
Shahany, L. — VIII-10
Shaitanka, R. — IV-2
Shakhe, R. — X-20
Shakhtars'ke — V-19; Db III-4
Shakhtars'ke, Dn — IV-2
(Shakhtars'ke) Petropavlivka — V-17
Shakhtne, Dn — IV-4
Shakhty (Aleksander Grushevskii) — IV-21; Db IV-8
Shalaivka — IV-22
Shali — X-26
Shalyhyne — II-15
Shamkhal — X-28
Shamraivka — IV-10
Shapsuhs'ke Res. — IX-19

Shapsukho, R. *IX-19*
Sharashova *I-5*
Sharhorod *V-9*
Sharivka *III-16*
Shats'k *II-4*
(Shatsilky) Svietlagors'k *I-10*
Shchara, R. *I-6*
Shchaslyva *IV-9*
Shchaslyvtseve *VII-15*
Shchastia *V-20; Db II-6*
Shchebetivka *IX-19*
Shchepynivka *III-17*
Shcherbakova *III-20*
Shcherbaky *VI-16*
Shcherbani *VI-12*
Shcherbanka *VII-11*
Shcherbynivka *Db III-3*
Shchigry *II-17*
Shchors (Snovs'ke) *II-12*
Shchors'ke (Bozhedarivka) *V-15*
Shchotove *V-20; Db III-6*
Shchyrets' *IV-4*
Shchyrets', R. *IV-4*
Shebekyne *III-17*
Shebelynka *IV-17*
Shebsh, R. *IX-19*
Shedok *IX-21*
Shelkovskaia *X-27*
Shepetivka *III-8*
Shessi, Mt. *IX-20*
Shevchenko *V-18; Db III-2*
Shevchenkove (Sm) *II-14*
Shevchenkove (Chrk) *IV-12*
Shevchenkove (Khrk) *IV-18*
Shevchenkove (Od) *VIII-10*
Shiriai, R. *IV-25*
Shklo *IV-4*
Shklo, R. *III-3*
Shkuryns'ka *VII-20*
Shliakhtova *IV-1*
Shpakovskoie *VIII-23*
Shpola *IV-12*
Shpolka, R. *IV-12*
Shpykiv *V-9*
Sholokhovskii *V-22*
Shostka *II-14*
Shostka, R. *II-14*
Shovgenovskii *VIII-21*
Shramkivka *III-13*
Shtepivka *III-15*
Shterivka, Dn *III-5*
Shtormove, Db *I-5*
Shtun' *II-5*
Shubivka *IV-11*
Shul'hivka *V-15*
Shul'hynka *IV-19; Db I-5*
Shuliaky *IV-10*
Shums'ke *III-7*
Shybena *IV-7*
Shylivka, Dn *III-1*
Shypuvate *IV-18*
Shypyntsi *V-6*
Shyriaieve *VI-11*
Shyrmivka *IV-10*
Shyroka Balka *VII-13*
Shyroke (Dnp) *VI-14*
Shyrokolanivka *VI-12*
Shyrokyne *VI-18*
Shyshaky *IV-15*
Siadryne *II-13*
Sian, R. *IV-3, III-3*
Sian Lowland *III-3*
Sianik (Sanok) *IV-3*
Sianky *IV-3*
Siedlce *I-3*
Siedove *VI-19*

Siemiatycze *I-3*
Sieniawa *III-3*
Şieu, R. *VI-5*
Şiev, R. *I-15*
(Sighetu Marmaţiei) *VI-4*
Sighişoara *VII-5*
Sil', Db *II-4*
Silistra *IX-8*
Simakivka *III-9*
Simeikine, Dn *III-7*
Simeiz *IX-15*
Simeria *VII-4*
(Sim Kolodiaziv) Lenine *VIII-16*
Şimleu Silvaniei *VI-3*
Şimonka, Mt. *V-2*
Sinaia *VIII-6*
Sinegorskii *V-21*
Sîngeorz-Băi *VI-5*
(Sîngerei) Lazovsk *VI-9*
Sinna *VIII-17*
Sinne *III-16*
Sinoie, L. *IX-9*
Siriu Mts. *VIII-7*
Siutghiol, L. *IX-9*
Sivashs'ke *VII-15*
Siverne *V-19; Db III-5*
Sivernyi *V-20; Db III-7*
Sivero-Hundorivs'kyi, Dn *III-7*
Sivers'ka *IX-19*
Sivers'kodonets'ke *V-19; Db II-4*
Skadovs'ke *VII-13*
Skala-Podil's'ka *V-7*
Skalat *IV-6*
Skaleva *V-11*
Skaryszew *II-2*
Skarzysko-Kamienna *II-1*
Skeliuvate, L. *VIII-19*
Skel'ky *VI-16*
Skhidnii Bulhanak, R *VIII-15*
Skhidnii Lim. *VIII-18*
Skhidnytsia *IV-4*
Skierniewice *II-1*
Skole *IV-4*
Skorodne *II-9*
Skosyrs'ka *V-22*
Skotuvata *V-18; Db III-3*
Skuraty *III-10*
Skynosa, R. *VII-9*
Skvyra *IV-10*
Skvyrka, R. *IV-10*
Slănic-Moldova *VII-7*
Slanske Mts. *IV-2*
Slatyne *III-17*
Slava, R. *IX-9*
Slavhorod (Sm) *III-16*
Slavhorod (Dnp) *V-16*
Slaviatychi *II-4*
Slavs'ke *V-4*
Slavuta *III-7*
Sliporid, R. *III-13*
Slobidka (Vlh) *III-26*
Slobidka (Od) *VI-10*
Slobids'ka Ukraine, hist. reg. *III-15*
Sloboda *I-9*
Sloboda-Rungurs'ka *V-5*
Slobodyshche *III-9*
Slobodzeia (Mol) *VII-10*
Slobozia *VI-8*
Slobozia *IX-8*
Slonivka *III-18*
Slonivka, R. *III-6*
Slot', R. *II-13*
Slout *II-14*
Slovak Ore Mts. *V-1*

Slovechna, R. *II-10*
Slovechne *II-9*
Slovechne-Ovruch Ridge *II-9*
Slovianka *V-17*
Slovianohirs'ke *IV-18; Db I-3*
Slovianoserbs'ke *V-19; Db II-5*
Slovians'k *VIII-19*
Slovians'ke *V-18; Db II-3*
Sluch, R. (Horyn) *IV-7, II-7*
Sluch, R. (Prypiat') *I-8*
Slutsk *0-8*
Smahliivka *IV-20*
Smerekovytsia, Mt. *IV-1*
Smiach, R. *II-12*
Smila *IV-12*
Smile *III-14*
Smolens'ka *IX-19*
Smolka, R. *III-8*
Smotrych *V-7*
Smotrych, R. *IV-7*
Smotryky *III-13*
Smychyn *II-12*
Snezhet', R. *0-15*
Sniatyn *V-6*
Snihurivka *VI-13*
Snitkiv *V-8*
Snizhne *V-19; Db III-5*
Snov, R. *I-13, II-12*
Snova, R. (Don) *I-19*
Snova, R. (Tuskor) *I-17*
Snovs'ke (Shchors) *II-12*
Snyna *V-3*
Snyvoda, R. *IV-9*
Sob, R. *IV-10*
Sobolivka (Zht) *III-10*
Sobolivka (Vn) *V-10*
Sobrance *V-3*
Sobych *II-14*
Sochaczew *I-1*
Sochi *X-20*
Sochi, R. *X-20*
Sofiivka, Dn *II-3*
Sofiivka (Mk) *V-12*
Sofiivka (Dnp) *V-14*
Sofiivs'kyi *V-19; Db III-5*
Sokal' *III-5*
Sokil'nyky *IV-4*
Sokolovo-Kundriuchens'kyi *VI-20; Db IV-7*
Sokołów Małopolski *III-3*
Sokołów Podliaski *I-3*
Sokyriany *V-8*
Solca *VI-6*
Soldats'ke *III-16*
Solenyi *VI-21*
Solntsevo *II-17*
Solobkivtsi *IV-7*
Solodkyi Lim. *VII-19*
Solodkyi Lim. *VIII-18*
Solokiia, R. *III-4*
Solomna *IV-7*
Solona, R. (Bazavluk) *VI-15*
Solona, R. (Vovcha) *V-17; Db III-1*
Solone *V-15*
Solone Ozero *VIII-15*
Solonets' *VI-6*
Solontsi *IV-19*
Solonytsivka *IV-17*
Solotvyna (Zk) *VI-4*
Solotvyna (IF) *V-5*
Solynka *IV-3*
Solynka, R. *IV-3*
Solynka Res. *IV-3*
Someş, R. *VI-4*
Someş Upland *VI-4*

Someş Lowland *VI-3*
Someşul Cald, R. *VII-3*
Someşul Mare, R. *VI-5*
Someşul Mic, R. *VI-4*
Someşul, Rece, R. *VII-4*
Somovo *II-20*
Soniachna Dolyna *IX-16*
Sontsedar *IX-19*
Sopych *II-15*
Sorokoshychi *II-11*
Soroky *V-9*
(Sorokyne) Krasnodon *V-20*
Sosna, R. *I-17, I-19*
Sosnivka (Sm) *II-14*
Sosnivka (Lv) *III-5*
Sosnove *III-7*
Sosnovytsia *II-4*
Sosnytsia *II-13*
Sostinskoie, L. *VIII-26*
Sosyk, R. *VII-12*
Sosyka, R. *VII-21*
Sotnykivka *III-12*
Southern Carpathians *VIII-5*
Sovata *VII-6*
Sovetskaia *IX-22*
Soviets'ke (Blh) *III-19*
Sovietskoie (Kal) *VI-25*
Sovetskoie (K-BO) *X-24*
Soviets'kyi (Ishky) *VIII-15*
Sovytsia, R. *V-6*
Sozh, R. *0-11, I-11*
Spas *IV-3*
Spas'ke (Dnp) *V-16*
Spasskoie (St) *VIII-24*
Spišská Belá *IV-1*
Spišská Nová Ves *V-1*
Spišská Stará Ves *IV-1*
Spivakivka *IV-19; Db I-5*
Spokoinaia *IX-22*
Sporivs'ke, L. *I-6*
Sred. Akhtuba *V-25*
Sribne, Dn *III-1*
Sribne (Chrh) *III-13*
Staiky *III-11*
Stakhanov (Kadiivka) *V-19; DbII-5*
Stalowa Wola *III-3*
Stanovaia Riasa, R. *0-20*
Stanychne *IV-16*
Stanychno-Luhans'ke *V-20; Db II-7*
Stanyslav *VII-13*
Stanyslavchyk *III-5*
Stanyslavchyk *V-9*
(Stanysliaviv) Ivano-Frankivs'ke *V-5*
Stanyslaviv Basin *V-5*
Starachowice *II-2*
Stara Huta *I-14*
Stara Kotel'nia *III-9*
Stara Kriusha *III-22*
Stará L'ubovňa *IV-1*
Stara Maiachka *VII-14*
Stara Milova *III-21*
Stara Moshchanytsia *III-7*
Stara Orzhytsia *III-12*
Stara Poltavka *III-27*
Stara Riasna *I-4*
Stara Sil' *IV-3*
Stara Syniava *IV-8*
Stara Ushytsia *V-8*
Stara Vyzhivka *II-5*
Starchenkove *VI-17*
Stare, L. *VIII-14*
Stare Selo (Rv) *II-8*
Stare Selo (Lv) *IV-5*
Starobesheve *VI-19; Db IV-4*
Starobil's'ke *IV-19; Db I-5*

25

Starobin	I-8
Starodub	I-13
Starokorsuns'ka	VIII-20
Starokostiantyniv	IV-8
Starokozache	VII-10
Staroleushkivs'ka	VIII-20
Staromins'ka	VII-20
Staromlynivka	VI-17
Staromykhailivka	Db III-3
Staromyshastivs'ka	VIII-20
Staronyzhniostebliv'ska	VIII-19
Staroshcherbynivs'ka	VII-19
Starotytarivs'ka	VIII-18
Starovelychkivs'ka	VIII-19
Starovirivka	IV-16
Stary Sącz	IV-1
Staryi Chortoryis'k	II-6
Staryi Dykiv	III-3
Staryi Krym (Dnts)	VI-18
Staryi Krym (Krm)	VIII-16
Staryi Kryvyn	III-7
Staryi Merchyk	IV-16
Staryi Mizun'	V-4
Staryi Oskol	II-18
Staryi Ostropil'	IV-8
Staryi Saltiv	III-17
Staryi Sambir	IV-3
Staryi Terek, R.	X-27
Starie Darogy	0-9
Starytsia	III-17
Staszów	III-2
Stavky	VI-12
Stavne	V-3
Stavropil' Region, hist. reg.	IX-23
Stavropol'	VII-23
Stavropol' Heighland	VIII-22
Stavrove	VI-10
Stavy	IV-11
Stavy, R.	III-7
Stavyshche	IV-11
Stebliv	IV-12
Stebnyk	IV-4
Stefanivka	VI-8
Steniatyn	III-5
Stepan'	II-7
Stepanhorod	II-7
Stepanivka (Sm)	III-15
Stepanivka, Dn	IV-5
Stepanivka (Krv)	V-13
Stepanivka (Dnts)	V-18; Db II-2
Stepano-Krynka, Dn	IV-4
Stepantsi	IV-12
Stepashky	V-10
Stepna	VIII-19
Stepne (St)	IX-25
Stepne, Dn	IV-3
Steppe Nat. Res.	VII-25
Stetseva	V-6
Stetsivka	IV-13
Stets'kivka	II-15
Stih, Mt.	V-4
Stînişoara Mts.	VI-6
Stobykhva	II-6
Stoczek Łukowski	II-2
Stodolychi	II-9
Stoianiv	III-5
Stokhid, R.	II-6
Stolyn	II-7
Storozhynets'	V-6
Stradech	II-4
Strășeni	VI-9
Stratiivka	V-10
Striatyn	IV-5
Strileckyi Step, Res.	IV-21
Strilky	IV-3

Stril'nyky	II-14
Stril'tsivka	IV-20
Stroitel'	III-17
Stropkov	IV-2
Struha	V-8
Strusiv	IV-6
Strybizh	III-9
Stryi	IV-4
Stryi, R.	IV-5
Strypa, R.	IV-6
Stryvihor, R.	IV-3
Stryzhament, Mt	IX-23
Stryzhavka	IV-9
Stryzów	IV-2
Stubazka, R.	III-6
Stubla, R.	II-7
Studenok, Db	I-2
Studenytsia	V-7
Studenytsia, R.	V-7
Stuhna, R.	III-11
Stvyha, R.	II-8
Styla, Dn	IV-3
Styr, R.	III-5, II-6
Subcarpathia, geogr. reg.	IV-4
Subcaucasia, geogr. reg.	VIII-20
Subotiv	IV-13
Subottsi	V-13
Suceava	VI-7
Suceava, R.	VI-6
Suchedniów	II-1
Sudak	IX-15
Sudost', R.	0-14
Sudova Vyshnia	IV-4
Sudylkiv	III-8
Sudzha	II-16
Sudzha, R.	II-16
Suhaia, L	X-6
Suiutkina Spit	IX-28
Sukha, R.	X-8
Sukha Volnovakha, R.	VI-18; Db IV-3
Sukhi Yaly, R.	VI-18; Db IV-2
Sukhoi	VI-22
Sukhokliia, R.	V-12
Sukhyi Lyman	VII-11
Sukhyi Tashlyk, R.	V-12
Sukhyi Torets', R.; Db II-2	V-17
Sukhyi Yelanchyk, R.	VI-19, Db IV-4
Sukhyi Yelanets'	VI-12
Sukil, R.	IV-4
Sula, R.	III-15, IV-13
Sulak	X-28
Sulak, R.	X-28
Sulejów	II-0
Sulejówek	I-2
Sulina (Sulyn)	VIII-10
Sulina Estuary	VIII-10
Sultans'ke	IX-23
Sulyns'kyi, Dn	IV-8
Sumy	III-15
Sunky	IV-13
Sunzha, R.	X-25
Sunzha Range	X-25
Supii, R.	III-12
Surazh (Brn)	0-13
Surazh (Tr)	III-7
Surovikino	V-23
Sușița, R.	VII-7
Sutkivtsi	IV-7
Suvorove (Dnp)	VI-14
Suvorove (Mol)	VII-10
Suvorove (Od)	VIII-9
Suvorovs'ka	IX-23

Suzemka	I-15
Svaliava	V-3
Svapa, R.	II-15
Svarytsevychi	II-7
Svatove	IV-19
Sved, R.	I-10
Sverdlove (Od)	VII-11
Sverdlovs'ke	V-20; Db III-7
Sverdlykove	II-16
Svesa	II-14
Svetlii Yar	V-25
Svetlograd (Petrovskoie)	VIII-23
Svetloie, L.	VIII-26
Sviata Volia	I-6
Sviatohorivka, Dn	III-2
Svicha, R.	V-4, IV-5
Svietlahorsk (Shatsilky)	I-10
Svirzh, R.	IV-5
Svishtov	X-6
Svitlodars'ke, Dn	III-4
Svitlovods'ke (Kremhes)	IV-14
Svobody	IX-24
Svydivok	IV-12
Svydnyk	IV-2
Svydovets', R.	II-9
Svyha, R.	I-14
Svynia, R.	III-4
Svyten'ka, R.	III-7
Svytiaz'	II-4
Svytiaz', L.	II-4
Svynkivka, R.	IV-15
Świder R.	I-2
Swidnik	II-3
Sydorivka	II-13
Syhit (Sighetu Marmaţiei)	VI-4
Symferopil'	IX-15
Symonovychi	II-9
Synel'nykove	V-16
Synevyr	V-4
Synevyr, L.	V-4
Syniak, Mt.	V-3
Syniava	IV-11
Syniukha, R. (Boh)	V-11
Syniukha, R. (Kuban')	IX-22
Syniukhyn Brid	V-11
Synytsia, R.	V-11
Syren', R.	II-7
Syrotyne	V-19; Db II-5
Syrovatka, R.	III-16
Syrove	VI-11
Syrskii	I-20
Sytkivtsi	V-10
Sytniaky	III-10
Syvash L.	VII-14
Syvka, R.	IV-5
Syvulia, Mt	V-5
Szamos, R.	VI-3
Szczawnica	IV-1
Szeghalom	VI-2
Szczebrzeszyn	III-3
Szikszó	V-1
Szreniawa, R.	III-1
Szydlowiec	II-1

T

Tahamlyk, R.	IV-15
Tahanrih	VI-19
Tahanrih Bay	VII-18
Tai-Koba, Mt.	IX-15
Taina, R.	IV-6
Taita, R.	VIII-9
Talakivka	VI-18

Talalaivka	III-14
Talivka	V-21
Tal'ne	V-11
Talovaia	II-21
Talove	V-20; Db III-7
Talovii	VI-21
Taly	IV-21
Taman'	VIII-17
Taman' Bay	VIII-17
Taman' Pen.	VIII-17
Tambov	I-22
Ţăndărei	IX-8
Tanev, R.	III-4
Taraclia	VIII-9
Tarashcha	IV-11
Tarasivka (Pl)	III-15
Tarasivka (Vr)	IV-19
Tarasivs'kyi	V-21
Tarcău Mts.	VII-7
Tarczyn	II-1
Tarkhankut, C.	VIII-13
Tarkhankut Upland	VIII-13
Tarky	XI-28
Tarnobrzeg	III-2
Tarnohorod (Tarnogród)	III-3
(Tarnogród)	III-3
Tarnów	III-1
Taroms'ke	V-15
Tartakiv	III-5
Tarumovka	IX-27
Tarutyne	VII-10
Tashan'	III-12
Tashchenak, R.	VII-16
Tashlyk	IV-12
Tashyne	VII-12
Tăşnad	VI-3
Tatarbunary	VIII-10
Tatsinskii	V-22
Tavriis'ke	VII-14
Tazlău, R.	VII-7
Tbiliskaia	VIII-21
Teberda	X-22
Teberda, R.	X-22
Teberda Res.	X-22
Techirghiol	IX-9
Tecuci	VIII-8
Teleajen, R.	VIII-6
Telekhany	I-6
Teleneşti	VI-9
Teleorman, R.	IX-6
Teliţa, R.	VIII-9
Tel'manove	VI-19
Temirgoievskaia	VIII-21
Temriuk	VIII-18
Temriuk Bay	VIII-18
Tendriv Bay	VII-12, 13
Tendriv Spit	VII-12
Teodosiia Bay	VIII-16
Teodosiia	VIII-16
Teofipil'	IV-7
Tepla, R. Db	II-6
Teplyk	V-10
Teplytsi	III-3
Terbuny	I-19
Tereblia, R.	V-4
Terebovlia	IV-6
Terek Range	X-25
Terek, R.	X-25, X-27
Terek	X-25
Terek-Kuma Can.	IX-25
Terek-Kuma Lowland	IX-25
Terek Region	X-24
Teremtsi	II-11
Tereshpil'	IV-8
Terespil'	I-4
Teresva	V-4
Teresva, R.	V-4

Termakhivka	*II-10*		
Tern, R.	*II-14*		
Ternava, R.	*V-7*		
Ternivka (Vn)	*V-10*		
Ternivka (Krv)	*V-11*		
Ternivka (Dnp)	*V-17*		
Ternivka (Mk)	*VI-13*		
Ternivka, R.	*V-17*		
Ternopil'	*IV-6*		
Ternove	*V-4*		
Ternuvate	*VI-17*		
Terny, Db	*I-3*		
Terny (Sm)	*III-14*		
Terny (Dnp)	*V-14*		
Terpinnia	*VII-16*		
Tervel	*X-8*		
Teteriv, R.	*IV-8, III-10*		
Tetiiv	*IV-10*		
Teuz, R.	*VII-2*		
Tevli	*I-5*		
Thorez	*V-19; Db III-5*		
Tiachiv	*V-4*		
Tiahynka	*VII-14*		
Tiasmyn, R.	*IV-13*		
Ţibleş, Mt.	*VI-5*		
Ţibleş Mts.	*VI-5*		
(Tighina) Bendery	*VII-10*		
Tikhaia, R.	*IV-22*		
Tikhaia Sosna, R.	*III-19*		
Tikhoretsk	*VIII-21*		
Tim	*II-18*		
Tim, R.	*II-18*		
Timiş, R.	*VIII-2*		
Tirgovişte	*IX-6*		
Tîrgu Bujor	*VIII-8*		
Tîrgu Frumos	*VI-7*		
Tîrgu Lăpuş	*VI-4*		
Tîrgu Mureş	*VII-5*		
Tîrgu-Neamţ	*VI-7*		
Tîrgu Ocna	*VII-7*		
Tîrgu Secuisc	*VII-7*		
Tîrnava Mare, R.	*VII-4*		
Tîrnava Mica, R.	*VII-4*		
Tîrnava, R.	*VII-4*		
Tîrnava Upland	*VII-5*		
Tîrnăveni	*VII-5*		
Tisa Lowland	*V-2*		
Tishanka, R. (Don)	*IV-25*		
Tishanka, R. (Medvedytsia)	*III-24*		
Tiszalók	*V-2*		
Tiszavasvári	*VI-2*		
Titchyne	*II-15*		
Titu	*IX-6*		
Tiulenii, Isl.	*IX-28*		
Tkhab, Mt.	*IX-19*		
(Tlumach) Tovmach	*V-5*		
Tłushch	*I-2*		
Tnia, R.	*III-9*		
Tobechyls'ke, L.	*VIII-17*		
Toboly	*II-6*		
Tochylove	*VI-10*		
Tokai, R.	*II-21*		
Tokaj	*V-2*		
Tokarevka	*II-22*		
Tokmak	*VI-16*		
Tokmak, R.	*VI-16*		
Tolbukhin (Dobrych)	*X-8*		
Tolucheievka, R.	*III-21*		
Tomakivka	*VI-15*		
Tomakivka, R.	*VI-15*		
Tomarovka	*III-17*		
Tomashhorod	*II-8*		
Tomashivka	*II-4*		
Tomashivtsi	*IV-5*		
Tomashpil'	*V-9*		
Tomaszów	*III-4*		
Tomaszów Mazowiecki	*II-1*		
Tomuzlovka, R.	*IX-24*		
Tonizh	*II-8*		
Topl'a, R.	*IV-2*		
Topliţa	*VII-6*		
Topoloveni	*IX-6*		
Toporiv	*III-5*		
Toporivtsi	*V-7*		
Torchyn	*III-5*		
Torgun, R.	*III-28*		
Torhove	*VI-24*		
Torhovytsia	*V-11*		
Toroiaga, Mt.	*VI-5*		
Torysa, R.	*IV-1*		
Toshkivka, Dn	*II-5*		
Tovkachivka	*III-13*		
Tovmach	*V-12*		
Tovmach (Tlumach)	*V-5*		
Tovste	*V-6*		
Tovtry, geogr. reg.	*IV-6*		
Trakhtemyriv	*IV-12*		
Transilvania, hist. reg.	*VII-4*		
Transilvanian Basin	*VII-4*		
Transcarpathia, hist. reg.	*V-3*		
Trascău Mts.	*VII-2*		
Trebišov	*V-2*		
Tremlia, R.	*I-9*		
Troianiv	*III-9*		
Troianivka	*II-6*		
Troïts'ka	*VIII-19*		
Troïts'ke Dn	*II-4*		
Troïts'ke (Vr)	*IV-19*		
Troïts'ke (Od)	*VI-11*		
Troitskoie (Kal)	*VII-25*		
Troïts'ko-Khartsyz'ke	*VI-19; Db IV-4*		
Troïts'ko-Safonove	*VI-13*		
Tr'okhizbenka	*V-19; Db II-5*		
Troshcha	*IX-9*		
Trostianets' (Vl)	*III-6*		
Trostianets' (Sm)	*III-15*		
Trostianets' (Vn)	*V-9*		
Trostianets' (Vn)	*V-10*		
Trostianets', R.	*VI-10*		
Trostianytsia, R.	*III-9*		
Trotuş, R.	*VII-7*		
Trubchevsk	*I-14*		
Trubizh, R. (Dnieper)	*III-12*		
Trubizh, R. (Snov)	*I-13*		
Trudfront	*VIII-28*		
Trudove	*VIII-10*		
Trudy, R.	*I-18*		
Truskavets'	*IV-4*		
Tryduby	*V-11*		
Trykhaty	*VI-12*		
Trykraty	*VI-12*		
Trylisy	*IV-10*		
Trypillia	*III-11*		
Tsahan Aman	*VI-27*		
Tsareha, R.	*VI-12*		
Tsaritsa, R.	*IV 23*		
Tsarychanka	*V-15*		
Tsaryns'ka, Mt.	*V-3*		
(Tsarytsyn) Volgohrad	*V-25*		
Tsebrykove	*VI-11*		
Tselina	*VII-22*		
Tsemes'ka Bay	*IX-18*		
Tserakhovka	*I-12*		
Tserem, R.	*III-8*		
Tsetsyna, Mt.	*V-6*		
Tshchyts'ke Res.	*VIII-20*		
Tsiarukha, R.	*I-12*		
Tsiata, R.	*I-12*		
Tsimla, R.	*V-23*		
Tsimliansk	*VI-23*		
Tsimliansk Res.	*V-23*		
Tsiurupyns'ke	*VII-13*		
Tsna, R. (Moksha)	*I-22*		
Tsna, R. (Prypiat')	*I-7*		
Tsokur Lim.	*VIII-17*		
Tson, R.	*I-16*		
Tsukhovyi Dil, Mt.	*IV-4*		
Tsukrova Holova, Mt.	*IX-18*		
Tsukuryne	*V-18; Db III-2*		
Tsuman'	*III-6*		
Tsutskan, R.	*IV-23*		
Tsvitkove	*IV-12*		
Tsvitne	*V-13*		
Tsvitokha, R.	*III-7*		
Tsybuliv	*IV-10*		
Tsybulnyk, R.	*V-13*		
Tsyr (Breshcha) R.	*II-5*		
Tsyrkuny	*III-17*		
Tsytsiv	*II-4*		
Tuapse	*IX-20*		
Tuapse, R.	*IX-20*		
Tuby	*IX-20*		
Tuchów	*IV-2*		
Tuchyn	*III-7*		
Tukhlia	*V-4*		
Tukhol'ka	*V-4*		
Tulcea	*VIII-9*		
Tul'chyn	*V-9*		
Tul's'kyi	*IX-21*		
Tumak	*VII-29*		
Tupychiv	*II-12*		
Tupyi, Mt.	*V-4*		
Tur, R.	*VI-4*		
Tur, L.	*II-5*		
Turbiv	*IV-9*		
Turda	*VII-4*		
Turia, R.	*V-3*		
Turiia Can.	*II-5*		
Turiia, R.	*II-5*		
Turiis'ke	*II-5*		
Turiv	*I-8*		
Turi Remety	*V-3*		
Turka	*IV-4*		
Turkovychi	*III-4*		
Tuskor, R.	*II-17*		
Tutova, R.	*VII-8*		
Tutrakan	*IX-7*		
Ţuţora	*VI-8*		
Ţuţuiat, Mt.	*VIII-9*		
Tuzliv, R.	*VI-20; Db IV-6*		
Tuzly	*VIII-11*		
Tychyn	*IV-3*		
Tyliava	*IV-2*		
Tylihul Lim.	*VII-12*		
Tylihul, R.	*VI-11*		
Tylych	*IV-2*		
Tylych Pass	*IV-2*		
Tymanivka	*V-9*		
Tymashivs'k	*VIII-19*		
Tymchenky	*IV-13*		
Tymkove	*VI-10*		
Tymonove	*IV-19*		
Tymoshivka	*VI-16*		
Tynivka	*IV-11*		
Tynne	*II-7*		
Tyraspil'	*VII-10*		
Tyrava Volos'ka	*IV-3*		
Tyrnyauz	*X-23*		
Tysa, R.	*V-4, VI-2*		
Tyshkivka	*V-11*		
Tys'menytsia	*V-5*		
Tys'menytsia R.	*IV-4*		
Tysmienica, R.	*II-3*		
Tyshivtsi	*III-4*		
Tysna	*IV-3*		
Tyvriv	*IV-9*		
U			
Ubid', R.	*II-13*		
Ublia	*V-3*		
Ublia, R.	*II-18*		
Ubort', R.	*III-8, I-9*		
Ubynka, R.	*IX-19*		
Udachne, Db	*III-1*		
Udai, R.	*III-13*		
Udarnyi	*IX-23*		
Udobnaia	*IX-22*		
Udy	*III-17*		
Udy, R.	*III-16*		
Udych, R.	*V-10*		
Uglegorskii	*V-22*		
Uglerodovskii	*V-21; Db III-8*		
(Ugol'nyi)	*X-24*		
Uherka, R.	*II-4*		
Uhlia	*V-4*		
Uhniv	*III-4*		
Uhroïdy	*III-16*		
Uhrus'k	*II-4*		
Ujfehértó	*VI-2*		
Ukraïnka (Kv)	*III-11*		
Ukraïnka (Krm)	*IX-15*		
Ukrains'ke	*V-18; Db III-2*		
Ulan Khol	*VIII-27*		
Ulaniv	*IV-9*		
Ulanów	*III-3*		
Ulianivka (Sm)	*III-15*		
Ulianivka (Krv)	*V-11*		
Uliap	*VIII-20*		
Ulych	*V-3*		
Uman'	*V-11*		
(Umans'ka) Leninhrads'ka	*VII-20*		
Unava, R.	*IV-10*		
Unecha	*I-13*		
Unecha, R.	*I-13*		
Ungheni	*VI-8*		
Upper Buh R. Basin	*III-5*		
Upper Dniester Basin	*IV-4*		
Uraieva, R.	*III-19*		
Uralo-Kavkaz, Db	*III-7*		
Uralove	*I-14*		
Urazove	*III-19*		
Urda	*V-28*		
Urechcha	*I-8*		
Urlaţi	*VIII-7*		
Urozhaine	*IX-25*		
Ursus	*I-1*		
Urukh, R.	*X-25*		
Urup	*X-22*		
Urup, R.	*IX-22*		
Urup, Mt.	*X-22*		
Urziceni	*IX-7*		
Ushakivka, Dn	*II-7*		
Usman'	*I-20*		
Usman', R.	*II-20*		
Usok	*II-14*		
Usozha, R.	*I-16*		
Usozha, R. (Nerusa)	*I-15*		
Uspenivka, Dn	*IV-2*		
Uspenivka (Zp)	*VI-17*		
Uspenka (Sm)	*II-14*		
Uspenka, Dn	*IV-5*		
Uspenka (Vr)	*V-20; Db III-6*		
Uspenskaia	*VIII-22*		
Ust'-Chorna	*V-4*		
Ust'-Dzhehutyns'ka	*IX-22*		
Ust'-Labyns'k	*VIII-20*		
(Ust'-Medvedetskaia)	*IV-23*		
Ustens'ke Druhe (Derman')	*III-7*		
Ustia, R.	*III-7*		
Ustia Rus'ke	*IV-2*		
Ustia-Zelene	*IV-5*		
Ustryky Dolishni (Ustrzyki Dolne)	*IV-3*		
(Ustrzyki Dolne) Ustryky Dolishni	*IV-3*		
Ustyluh	*III-5*		

Ustynivka	VI-13
Ustyvytsia	IV-14
Utkivka	IV-17
Utliuk Lim.	VII-16
Uts', R.	I-12
Uvaravichy	I-11
Uza, R.	I-11
Uzh, R. (Liatorytsia)	V-3
Uzh (Usha), R.	II-9, II-10
Uzhhorod	V-3
Uzhok Pass	V-3
Uzhok	V-3
Uzunlars'ke, L.	VIII-17
Uzyn	IV-11

V

Vablia, R.	I-13
Vaha, R.	I-12
Vakhnivka	IV-9
Vakhrusheve	V-19; Db III-5
Vakulivka	III-20
(Valea Vişeului)	VI-5
Vălenii de Munte	VIII-7
Valky	IV-16
Vallachia, Hist. Reg.	IX-6
Valui, R.	III-19
Valuiky	III-19
Valuis'ke, Dn	II-7
Valuivka	VII-24
Valu-lui-Voda	VI-10
Vanchyn, Mt.	V-6
Van'kova	IV-3
Vapniarka	V-9
Vara, R.	I-14
Varenykivs'ka	VIII-18
Varkovychi	III-6
Varnavyns'ke Res.	VIII-19
Varva	III-13
Varvarivka, Dn	I-4
Varvarivka (Blh)	III-19
Varvarivka (Pl)	IV-16
Varvarivka (Dnp)	V-16
Vascău	VII-3
Vashkivtsi	V-6
Vashkivtsi	V-8
Vasilevichy	I-10
Vasiuryns'ka	VIII-20
Vas'kovychi	II-9
Vaslui	VII-8
Vaslui, R.	VII-8
Vasylivka (Sm)	III-15
Vasylivka (Krv)	V-14
Vasylivka (Zp)	VI-16
Vasylivka (Krm)	VIII-15
Vasyl'kiv	III-11
Vasyl'kivka	V-17
Vasyl'kivtsi	IV-7
Vasyshcheve	IV-17
Vatra Dornei	VI-6
Vatutine	IV-12
Vchoraishe	IV-10
Vedea, R.	X-6
Vedrach, R.	I-11
Veduga, R.	II-19
Veidelivka	III-19
Veliatyn	V-4
Velké Kapušany	V-3
Velychaivskoie	IX-26
Vel. Bahachka	IV-14
Vel. Berezna	III-8
Vel. Berezovytsia	IV-6
Vel. Bilozerka	VI-15
Vel. Bereznyi	V-3
Vel. Birky	IV-6
Vel. Blahovishchenka	VII-15
Vel. Bobryk	III-16

Vel. Budyshcha	III-15
Vel. Buhaivka	III-11
Vel. Burluk	III-18
Vel. Burluk, R.	IV-18
Vel. Bychkiv	VI-5
Vel. Chernihivka	V-20; Db II-6
Vel. Chornokintsi	V-7
Vel. Chuluk, R.	VI-9
Vel. Dal'nyk	VII-11
Vel. Dederkaly	III-7
Vel. Derevychi	IV-8
Vel. Dil, Mt.	III-4
Vel. Dil, Mts.	V-3
Vel. Dobron'	V-3
Vel. Dymerka	III-11
Vel. Dzhalha	VIII-23
Vel. Hlushcha	II-6
Vel. Hlybichok	IV-6
Vel. Horodyshche	III-18
Vel. Kalha, R.	VII-15
Vel. Kamianka	V-6
Vel. Kamianka, R.	V-20; Db III-6
Vel. Karasivka, R.	VIII-15
Vel. Katlabukh, R.	VIII-9
Vel. Khalan'	III-18
Vel. Kisnytsia	V-9
Vel. Kokhnivka	IV-14
Vel. Komyshuvakha, Db	I-1
Vel. Kopani	VII-13
Vel. Korenykha	VII-12
Vel. Korovyntsi	IV-9
Vel. Kostromka	VI-14
Vel. Kripka	VI-20; Db IV-6
Vel. Krynky	IV-14
Vel. Kuchuriv	V-6
Vel. Kuial'nyk, R.	VI-11
Vel. Kursanivka, Dn	IV-5
Vel. Laba, R.	X-21
Vel. Lepetykha	VI-14
Vel. Liubin'	IV-4
Vel. Loh	V-20; Db III-7
Vel. Luchky	V-3
Vel. Lypnyk	IV-1
Vel. Mezhyrichi	III-7
Vel. Mosty	III-5
Vel. Motykaly	I-4
Vel. Mykhailivka	VI-10
Vel. Nesvitai, R. Db	IV-7
Vel. Novosilka	VI-17
Vel. Ochi	III-4
Vel. Oleksandrivka	VI-14
Vel. Pysarivka	III-16
Vel. Radvanychi	I-5
Vel. Rostivka	IV-10
Vel. Rublivka	IV-15
Vel. Sambir	II-4
Vel. Sirohozy, R.	VII-15
Vel. Sorochyntsi	III-14
Vel. Topal'	I-13
Vel. Troits'ke	III-18
Vel. Turia	IV-5
Vel. Utliuk, R.	VII-15
Vel. Vil'shanka	III-11
Vel. Vys', R.	V-12
Vel. Vys'ka	V-12
Vel. Zelenchuk, R.	X-22
Vel. Zhvanchyk	V-7
Velky Milič, Mt.	V-2
Velyka (Bol'shaia) R.	V-22
Velykoarkhanhel's'ke	III-21
Velykodolyns'ke	VII-11
Velykokomarivka	VI-10
Velykomykhailivka (Blh)	III-18
Velykomykhailivka (Dnp)	VI-17

Velykopolovets'ke	IV-10
Velykoryta	II-5
Velykoserbulivka	VI-12
Velymche	II-5
Vepryk	III-10
Vepr (Wieprz), R.	III-4, II-3
Vendychany	V-8
Verba (Vl)	III-5
Verba (Rv)	III-6
Verbliuzhka	V-13
Verbova, R.	V-8
Verbyns'kyi, Dn	IV-8
Verenchanka	V-6
Vereshytsia, R.	IV-4
Veresneve	III-6
Veresnia, R.	II-10
Veresoch	II-12
Verhuny	IV-13
Verkhivka	V-8
Verkhivnia	IV-10
Verkhivtseve	V-15
Verkhnaia Khava	II-20
Verkhnia Tersa, R.	VI-16
Verkhnia Khortytsia	VI-16
Verkhniachka	V-11
Verkhniakivs'kyi	IV-21
Verkhnia Makiivka	IV-22
Verkhnia Oril'ka	IV-17
Verkhnia Syrovatka	III-15
Verkhnie Synevids'ke	IV-4
Verkhnii Baskunchak	V-27
Verkhnii Byk	III-22
Verkhnii Dzynal, Mt.	X-23
Verkhnii Khomutets	VII-21
Verkhnii Mamon	III-21
Verkhnii Nahol'chyk, Db	III-6
Verkhnii Rohachyk	VI-15
Verkhni Lubianky	III-18
Verkhniobakans'kyi	IX-18
Verkhniodniprovs'ke	V-15
Verkhnioteple	V-20; Db II-6
Verkhovie	I-18
Verkhovychi	I-4
Verkhovyna (Zhabie)	V-5
Verkhy	II-6
Vertiivka	II-12
Vesela	VII-21
Vesela Dolyna	VII-10
Vesela Hora	V-20; Db II-6
Vesele (Sm)	II-15
Vesele (Zp)	VI-15
Veselovs'ke Res.	VI-22
Veselukha, R.	II-6
Veselyi	VI-21
Veselynivka	III-12
Veselynove	VI-12
Veshenskaia	IV-22
Vesztö	VII-2
Vetly	II-6
Vetlyn	III-3
Viazivnytsia	III-3
Viazivok	V-16
Vicha, R.	V-4
Victoria	VIII-5
Videle	IX-6
Vidomlia	I-4
Vietka	I-12
Vihor (Wiar), R.	IV-3
Viholat Res.	V-2
Viis'kove	V-16
Vikno	V-6
Viktorivka	VI-11
Vil'cha	V-6
Vil'hivka, R.	V-20; Db III-6
Viliia	III-7
Viliia, R.	III-6
Vil'khivka, Db	III-4

Vil'khova (Ol'khovaia), R.	V-21
Vil'khovatka	III-20
Vil'khovchyn	IV-21
Vil'khovets' (Chrk)	IV-11
Vil'khovets' (Khm)	V-8
Vil'khuvatka	III-18
Vilnians'ke	VI-16
Vil'nohirs'ke	V-15
Vil'shana (Chrh)	III-13
Vil'shana (Chrk)	IV-12
Vil'shana (Khrk)	IV-18
Vil'shanka (Vn)	V-9
Vil'shanka (Krv)	V-11
Vil'shanka, R.	IV-12
Vil'shany (Br)	I-8
Vil'shany (Khrk)	III-16
Vin'kivtsi	IV-8
Vinnytsia	IV-9
Virmens'ke	VII-14
Vişeu (Vyshava), R.	VI-5
Vişeu de Sus	VI-5
Vishnevka	IX-20
Vits', R.	II-10
Vlădeasa, Mt.	VII-3
Vladymyrivs'ka, Dn	IV-8
Vladyslavivka	VIII-16
Vlăhiţa	VII-6
Vlasivka (Krv)	IV-14
Vlasivka (Khrk)	IV-16
Vlazovychi	0-13
Vnukovychi	I-12
Vodiano-Loryne	VI-13
Vodians'ke	V-18; Db II-2
Vodorozdil	IX-23
Voikove, Dn	IV-4
Voikove (Krm)	VIII-14
Voikovs'kyi	VI-19; Db IV-4
Voiniv	VII-21
Voinyliv	IV-5
Voislavychi	III-4
Voinka	VIII-14
Volcanic Carpathian, Mts.	V-2
Volga, R.	III-26, VII-28
Volga Upland	V-25
Volga-Don Can.	V-24
Volgodonsk	VI-23
Volgograd (Tsarytsyn)	V-25
Volgograd Res.	IV-26
Volgo-Kaspiiskii	VII-28
Volhynia, hist. reg.	III-6
Volhynian Polissia, geogr. reg.	II-4
Volhynian Ridge	II-4
Volhynian Upland	III-5
Volians'ke, L.	II-5
Vol'na	X-20
Volnovakha	VI-18; Db IV-2
Vol'nyi	VIII-26
Volochys'ke	IV-7
Volodarka	IV-10
Volodars'ke	V-20; Db III-7
Volodars'ke	VI-18
Volodars'ke-Volyns'ke	III-9
Volodarskii	VII-29
Volodava (Włodawa)	II-4
Volodymyrets'	II-7
Volodymyrivka (Dnts)	VI-18; Db IV-2
Volodymyrivka (Mk)	VI-11
Volodymyrivka (Mk)	VI-13
Volodymyr-Volyns'kyi	III-5
Volokhiv Yar	IV-17
Volokonivka	III-18
Volosan', Mt.	IV-3
Voloshyne	V-20; Db II-7
Volosivtsi	IV-8

Volos'ka Baklaliia   IV-18
Volos'ka Balakliika, R. IV-17
Voloskivtsi   II-13
(Volove)   V-4
Volovets'   V-4
Volovets', R.   V-7
Volovo   I-18
Volytsia   III-10
Volzhskii   V-25
Vontkivs'ka Magura, Mt.
    IV-2
Vorits'kyi Pass   V-4
Vorokhta   V-5
Vorona, R.   V-5
Vorone   IV-11
Voronezh   II-20
Voronezh, R.   I-20
Voronezh Nat. Res.   II-20
Voroniaky   IV-5
Voroniaky Upland   IV-6
Voronizh   II-14
Voroniz'ka   VIII-20
Voron'kiv   III-11
Voronkove   VI-10
Voronky   VIII-14
Voronok   I-13
Voronove, Dn   II-5
Voronovytsia   IV-9
Vorontsovka   III-21
(Vorontsovo-
Aleksandrovsk)   IX-24
Voroshylovhrad
(Luhans'ke)   V-20; Db II-6
Vorozhba (Sm)   II-15
Vorozhba (Sm)   III-15
Vorsklo, R.   III-17, V-15
Vorsklytsia, R.   III-16
Vorzel'   III-11
Voshyva, R.   IV-16
Voskhod   VI-22
Voskresens'ke   VI-13
Vostochnii Manych, R.
    VIII-25
Vovcha, R. (Donets') III-18
Vovcha, R. (Samara)
    V-18, V-16; Db III-2
Vovcha (Vovchans'ke) III-17
(Vovchans'ke)   III-17
Vovchans'ki Khutory III-18
Vovchans'kyi, Dn   III-8
Vovchoiarivka, Dn   II-4
Vovchukhiv   IV-4
Vovk, R.   IV-8
Vovkovyntsi   IV-8
Vovna   I-14
Vozdvyzhens'ke   VIII-24
Vozdvyzhivka   VI-17
Voznesenka   III-18
Voznesenka   VII-16
Voznesens'ke (Mk)   VI-12
Voznesens'ke (Chrk) IV-13
Voznesens'ke (St)   VIII-24
Voznia, R.   III-10
Vozsiiats'ke   VI-13
Vradiivka   VI-11
Vrancea Mts.   VIII-7
Vranov   V-2
Vrubivka, Dn   II-4
Vrubivs'kyi   V-20; Db III-6
Vuhledar, Dn   IV-2
Vuhlehirs'ke V-19; Db III-4
Vulcăneşti   VIII-9
Vuzlove   V-3
Vvedenka   IV-17
Vychivka   II-7
Vyhoda (I–F)   V-4
Vyhoda (Od)   VII-11
Vyhonivs'ke, L.   I-6

Vyhonoshchi   I-6
Vyhonychi   0-15
Vyhorlat, Mts.   V-2
Vyhorlat Res.   V-2
Vylkove   VIII-10
Vylok   V-3
Vynnyky   IV-5
Vynohradiv (Sevliush)   V-4
Vynohradove   VII-13
Vyr, R.   II-15
Vyry   II-15
Vys. Skalky, Mt.   IV-1
Vyselky   VIII-20
Vyshavs'ka Dolyna (Valea
Vişeului)   VI-5
Vyshche Solone   IV-18
Vyshenky   III-11
Vyshhorod   III-11
Vyshkiv Pass   V-4
Vyshkiv (Brn)   I-12
Vyshkiv (I-F)   V-4
Vyshneva   IV-18
Vyshneve, Dn   III-2
Vyshneve   III-11
Vyshnia, R.   IV-4
Vyshniaky   IV-14
Vyshnivchyk   IV-7
Vyshnivets'   IV-6
Vyshnivka (Mol)   VII-9
Vyslok Vel.   IV-2
Vysoke (Br)   I-4
Vysoke, Dn   IV-4
Vysoke (Chrh)   II-13
Vysoke (Kv)   IV-10
Vysokopillia   VI-14
Vysots'ke   II-7
Vysova   IV-2
Vystupovychi   II-10
Vysun', R.   VI-13
Vytachiv   III-11
Vytiazivka   V-12
Vytiazivs'kyi Lim.   VIII-18
Vyzhivka, R.   II-5
Vyzhnytsia   V-6

W

Warka   II-2
Warsaw   I-1
Węgrów   I-3
West Beskyds   IV-1
Western Carpathians   IV-1
Western Rumanian
Carpathians, Mts.   VII-3
Wieprz, R.   II-3
Wieprz-Krzna Can.   II-4
Wilga, R.   II-3
Wisfa, R.   III-1, I-1
Wisłoka, R.   IV-2
Wisłok, R.   III-3
(Włodawa)   II-4
Wołomin   I-2
Wschodnia, R.   III-1
Wysmierzyce   II-1
Wysznice   II-4
Wyszgród   I-1

Y

Yablona   VI-8
Yabloniv   V-5
Yablonivs'kyi   IX-19
Yablonovo   III-18
Yabluniv   IV-12
Yablunivka   III-13
Yablunyts'kyi Pass   V-5

Yahorlyk, R.   VI-10
Yahorlyts'kyi Lim.   VII-12
Yahotyn   III-12
Yakhnyky   III-14
Yakovlevo   III-17
Yakubiany   IV-1
Yakymivka   VII-16
Yalanets'   V-10
Yalanets', R.   V-10
Yalpukh, L.   VIII-9
Yalpukh, R.   VII-9
Yalpuzhel', R.   VII-9
Yalta (Dnts)   VII-18
Yalta (Krm)   IX-15
Yaltushkiv   V-8
Yama   V-19; Dn II-4
Yamne   III-16
Yampil' (Khm)   IV-7
Yampil' (Sm)   II-14
Yampil' (Vn)   V-9
Yampil' (Dnts) V-18; Db II-3
Yanchul, R.   VI-17
(Yaniv) Ivano-Frankove
    IV-4
Yantra, R.   X-6
(Yanushpil') Ivanopil'   IV-9
Yaremche   V-5
Yares'ky   IV-14
Yarhora   VII-9
Yarmolyntsi   IV-7
Yaroshivka   III-14
Yaroslavets'   II-14
Yaroslavskaia   IX-21
Yarova   IV-18; Db I-3
Yaruha   V-9
Yarun'   III-8
Yaryshiv   V-8
Yasel'da, R.   I-6
Yasen'   V-5
Yasen' Spit   VII-19
Yasenets', R.   II-9
Yaseniv Pil'nyi   V-6
Yasenivs'kyi   V-20; Db III-6
Yasens'ka   VII-19
Yashalta   VII-23
Yashchykove, Dn   III-5
Yashkul', R.   VII-25
Yashkul'   VII-26
Yasinia   V-5
Yaslys'ka   IV-2
Yasna Poliana, Dn   II-3
Yasne   IV-7
Yasnohirka   V-18; Db II-3
Yasnohorodka   III-11
Yastrubyne   II-15
Yasynivka   Db III-3
Yasynuvata   V-18; Db III-3
Yatran', R.   V-11
Yatranivka   V-11
Yavkyne   VI-13
Yavoriv   IV-4
Yavoriv   V-5
Yavoryna, Mt.   IV-1
Yefremov   0-19
Yefremovo-Stepanivka
    V-21
Yegorlyk, R.   IX-22
Yehorlyts'ka   VII-21
Yeia, R.   VII-20
Yeia Spit   VII-19
Yeis'ke   VII-19
Yeis'ke Lim.   VII-19
Yeis'ke Ukriplennia   VII-19
Yekaterynivka   VII-19
Yelan', R.   II-22
Yelanets'   VI-12
Yelan'-Kolenovskii   II-22
Yelets   I-19

Yelisavetinskoie   VIII-24
Yelizarove   V-15
Yel's'ke   II-10
(Yelysavethrad)   V-13
Yelysavethradka   V-13
Yelysavetivka   VII-15
Yelysavetivka   VII-17
Yelysavetivka   VII-19
Yelysavetyns'ka   VIII-19
Yelyseivka   VI-17
Yemil'chyne   III-8
Yenakiieve   V-19; Db III-4
Yenotaievka   VI-28
Yepifanivka, Db   I-5
Yergeni Hills   VII-25
Yerkivtsi   III-12
Yerky   V-11
Yeruslan, R.   III-27
Yeryk, R. Db   II-5
Yesman', R. (Desna)   II-14
Yesman', R. (Kleven') II-14
Yevhenivka, Dn   IV-2
Yevpatoria   VIII-14
Yevstrativka   III-20
Yevsuh, R.   IV-20
Yevsuh   IV-20; Db II-6
Yezuch, R.   II-14
(Yezupil')   IV-5
Yosypivka   V-11
Yunakivka   II-16
Yunashly, R.   VI-16
Yunokomunarivs'ke
    V-19; Db III-4
Yurasivka   III-20
Yurchenkove   IV-18
Yurivka   IV-9
Yurivka, Dn   III-5
Yurivka (Dnp)   V-17
Yurkivka   IV-12
Yurove   II-8
Yuzhno-Sukhokumsk IX-26
Yuzhnyi   VI-22

Z

Zábala, R.   VIII-7
Żabno   III-1
Zabolotiv   V-6
Zabolottia   II-5
Zabuzhzhia   II-4
Zachepylivka   IV-16
Zadonsk   I-19
Zahiria (Zagórz)   IV-3
(Zagórz)   IV-3
Zahnitkiv   V-9
Zahoroddia, geogr. reg. I-5
Zaiache   III-17
Zaitseve   V-16
Zaitseve   V-19; Db III-4
Zakharivka (Krv)   V-12
(Zakharivka) Frunzivka
    VI-10
Zakhidne   II-12
Zakhidnii Bulhanak, R.
    IX-14
Zakhidn'okapital'na, Dn
    IV-7
Zakotne   IV-19
Zakroczym   I-1
Zălau   VI-4
Zalegoshch'   I-17
Zalishchyky   V-6
Zalisne, Dn   III-5
Zaliznyi Rih, C.   VIII-17
Zaliztsi   IV-6
Zaliznychne (Dnp)   VI-14
Zaliznychne (Zp)   VI-17

Zaliznychne (Od) _VIII-9_
Zamankul, Mt. _X-25_
Zamhlai _II-12_
(Zamość) Zamostia _III-4_
Zapadyntsi _IV-8_
Zapaliv _III-3_
Zaporizhzhia, Dn _III-5_
Zaporizhzhia
(Oleksandrivs'ke) _VI-16_
Zaporiz'ka _VIII-17_
Zapruddia _IV-11_
Zaprudy _I-5_
Zărand Mts. _VII-2_
Zarichanka _V-7_
Zarichne _II-7_
Zarizhne _IV-17_
Zărneşti _VIII-6_
Zarubyntsi (Zht) _III-10_
Zarubyntsi (Chrk) _IV-12_
Zarudyntsi _IV-10_
Zarvanytsia _IV-6_
Zasosna _III-19_
Zastavna _V-6_
Zaterechnyi _IX-26_
Zatoka _VII-11_
Zatyshshia _VI-1C_
Zavadiv _III-4_
Zavadivka _VI-11_
Zavallia _V-11_
Zavitne _VI-24_
Zavodskoi _V-21_
Zavorychi _III-12_
Zavydiv _III-5_
Zawichost _III-2_
Zbarazh _IV-6_
Zbii _IV-3_
Zborov (Slo) _IV-2_
Zboriv (Tr) _IV-6_
Zbruch, R. _V-7_
Zdolbuniv _III-7_
Zelechów _II-2_
Zegrze Res. _I-2_
Zelenchukskaia _X-22_
Zelene (Krv) _V-14_
Zelene (Dnp) _VI-14_
Zelenivka _VII-13_
Zelenodol's'ke _VI-14_

Zelenokumsk (Vorontsovo-
Aleksandrovsk) _IX-24_
Zeletin, R. _VII-8_
Zemlianky, Dn. _III-3_
Zempléni-Hegység Mts. _V-2_
Zernograd _VII-21_
(Zhabie) Verkhovyna _V-5_
Zhabynka _I-5_
Zhar, R. _IV-8_
Zharok, R. _IV-8_
Zhashkiv _IV-11_
Zhashkovychi _III-5_
Zhdanivka _V-19; Db III-4_
Zhdanivka _V-16_
Zhdanov (Mariiupil') _VI-18_
Zhdanove _V-15_
Zhegestiv _IV-1_
Zhelanne, Dn _III-2_
Zheleznogorsk _I-16_
Zheleznovodsk _IX-24_
Zheliabovka _VIII-15_
Zhenyshkivtsi _IV-8_
Zherdia _V-7_
Zherebets', R. (Dinets')
_IV-19; Db I-3_
Zherebets', R. (Konka)
_VI-16_
Zheriv, R. _II-9_
Zhirnov _V-22_
Zhlobin _I-11_
Zhmerynka _IV-9_
Zholon', R. _II-9_
Zhoriany _II-4_
Zhornyshche _IV-10_
(Zhovkva) Nesterov _III-4_
Zhovnyne _IV-13_
Zhovta, R. _V-14_
(Zhovta Rika) _V-14_
Zhovte _V-14_
Zhovte, Dn _II-6_
Zhovten' _VI-11_
Zhovten' (Yezupil') _IV-5_
Zhovti Vody (Zhovta Rika)
_V-14_
Zhovtneve (Khrk) _III-18_
Zhovtneve (Sm) _III-15_
Zhovtneve (Kv) _III-12_

Zhovtneve (Vl) _III-5_
Zhovtneve (Chrh) _II-13_
Zhovtneve (Zp) _VI-16_
Zhovtneve (Mk) _VI-11_
Zhovtneve (Pl) _IV-15_
Zhovtneve
(Bohoiavlens'ke) _VII-13_
Zhovtyi Yar _VIII-10_
Zhukovs'ke _VII-22_
Zhukyn _III-11_
Zhuravka (Rs) _IV-21_
Zhuravka (Chrk) _V-12_
Zhuravka, R. _VI-11_
Zhuravlivka _III-17_
Zhuravne _IV-5_
Zhuravs'ka _VIII-20_
Zhuravskoie _IX-24_
Zhuravytsia _IV-3_
Zhurivka _III-12_
Zhvan _V-8_
Zhvan, R. _V-8_
Zhvanchyk, R. _IV-7_
Zhvanets' _V-7_
Zhvyrka _III-5_
Zhydachiv _IV-5_
Zhydychyn _III-6_
Zhykhove _I-14_
Zhylyne _IV-20_
Zhytkavichy _I-8_
Zhytomyr _III-9_
Zhytomyr Polissia _III-8_
Ziatkivtsi _V-10_
Zid'ky _IV-17_
Zielonka _I-2_
Zimnicea _X-6_
Zin'kiv (Khm) _IV-8_
Zin'kiv (Pl) _III-15_
Ziudev, Isl. _VIII-28_
Ziuk, C. _VIII-17_
Zlatna _VII-4_
Zlazne _III-7_
Zlynka (Brn) _I-12_
Zlynka (Krv) _V-12_
Zmiievka _I-17_
Zmiiv _IV-17_
Zmiinyi Isl. _VIII-11_

Zmitniv _II-13_
Znamenivka _V-16_
Znamenka _I-22_
Znamianka _V-13_
Znamianka Druha _V-13_
Znob-Novhorods'ke _I-14_
Znobivka, R. _I-14_
Zolka, R. _X-24_
Zolochiv (Lv) _IV-5_
Zolochiv (Khrk) _III-16_
Zolota Balka _VI-14_
Zolota Lypa, R. _IV-5_
Zolote _V-19; Db II-5_
Zolote Pole _VIII-16_
Zolotnyky _IV-6_
Zolotolyn _II-7_
Zolotonosha _IV-13_
Zolotonoshka, R. _IV-13_
Zolotukhino _I-17_
Zolotyi Kolodiaz', Dn _II-2_
Zolotyi Potik _V-6_
Zorykivka _IV-20_
Zoryns'ke _V-19; Db III-5_
Zubkovychi _II-8_
Zubra, R. _IV-5_
Zuhres _V-19; Db III-4_
Zuia _VIII-15_
Zuia, R. _VIII-15_
Zuivka _V-19; Db III-4_
Zuivtsi _III-14_
Zusha, R. _O-18_
Zvanivka, Dn. _II-4_
Zvereve _V-21; Db III-8_
Zvenyhorod (Lv) _IV-5_
Zvenyhorod (Tr) _V-7_
Zvenyhorodka _IV-11_
(Zviahel') Novohrad-
Volyns'kyi _III-8_
Zwoleń _II-2_
Zybkove _V-14_
Żychlin _I-0_
Zymivnyky _VI-23_
Zymne _III-5_
Zymohiria _V-19; Db II-5_
Zymovyshche _II-11_
Żyrardów _I-1_